WOODBURNING
PROJECT & PATTERN TREASURY

WOODBURNING
PROJECT & PATTERN TREASURY
CREATE YOUR OWN PYROGRAPHY ART WITH 70 MIX-AND-MATCH DESIGNS

Deborah Pompano

Fox Chapel
PUBLISHING

DEDICATION

Reach high, for stars lie hidden in your soul,
Dream deep, for every dream precedes the goal.

Pamela Vaull Starr

I dedicate this book with love to my husband, Joe, my life's companion and helpmate, in gratitude for his constant love, support, and understanding.

And to our beautiful and cherished daughters, Rachel, Rebecca, and Laura, who have brought so much joy and love into our lives.

Most of all, with deep thankfulness for this opportunity to share my love of art and nature with others, I dedicate this book to:

God, the Artist
*You take the pen,
and the lines dance.
You take the flute,
and the notes shimmer.
You take the brush,
and the colours sing.
So all things have meaning and beauty,
in that space beyond time where you are.
How, then, can I hold back anything from you?*

— Dag Hammarskjold
"Markings"

ACKNOWLEDGMENTS

I would like to thank the following people without whom this book would never have been written:

My parents, Dorothy and Sidney Beller, for instilling in me a love of art, nature, music, and good books, and for nurturing my imagination.

My sisters, Margie Beller, Wendy Huntington, Laurie Sklar, and Sandy Miller—whose love, friendship, laughter, (and emails) have comforted and encouraged me throughout the years.

Peg Couch, my editor at Fox Chapel Publishing, for believing in me. Her insights, friendly encouragement, expert guidance, and patience made this book possible and have changed my life. And to Kerri Landis and the talented staff at Fox Chapel Publishing, who have turned my life's dream of writing a book into a reality.

Orchid Davis, for her warmth and generosity of spirit as a teacher, and for her inspiring example.

Robert Becker, editor of *Creative Woodwork and Crafts* and *Pure Inspiration* magazines, for his kindness, support, and encouragement.

And to my very talented "guinea pig" woodburning students in my classes at the wonderful John C. Campbell Folk School—their enthusiasm and feedback inspired me and gave me the confidence to write this book.

We will be known forever by the tracks we leave behind.

Native American Proverb

Woodburning Project & Pattern Treasury is an original work, first published in 2011 by Fox Chapel Publishing Company, Inc. The patterns contained herein are copyrighted by the author. Readers may make copies of these patterns for personal use. The patterns themselves, however, are not to be duplicated for resale or distribution under any circumstances. Any such copying is a violation of copyright law.

The ambrosia maple platter used in the woodburning "Harvest Time" on page 45 was created by Frank Penta, woodturning instructor at the John C. Campbell Folk School. All other round platters used in this book were created by Montzka Woodworking, Forest Lake, MN (tpmontzka@aol.com).

ISBN 978-1-56523-482-6

Library of Congress Cataloging-in-Publication Data

Pompano, Deborah.
Woodburning project & pattern treasury / Deborah Pompano.
    p. cm.
Includes index.
ISBN 978-1-56523-482-6 (pbk.)
1. Pyrography. 2. Pattern books. I. Title. II. Title: Woodburning project and pattern treasury.
TT199.8.P66 2011
745.51'4--dc22
                    2011012651

To learn more about the other great books from Fox Chapel Publishing, or to find a retailer near you, call toll-free 800-457-9112 or visit us at *www.FoxChapelPublishing.com*.

Note to Authors: We are always looking for talented authors to write new books in our area of woodworking, design, and related crafts. Please send a brief letter describing your idea to Acquisition Editor, 1970 Broad Street, East Petersburg, PA 17520.

Printed in China
First printing: October 2011

ABOUT THE ARTIST

I was very lucky to grow up in a large family with four sisters, in Norwich, Connecticut. My parents, Sidney and Dorothy Beller, were both creative people. Dad was a certified public accountant, but his real love was woodworking, and our entire basement was filled with saws and tools. He always had a project going, and he built everything from a cedar closet for our clothes to bookcases to a handsome inlaid map of the United States made from fifty different types of wood veneers! Dad's other loves were playing the piano and gardening. I am grateful to have inherited Dad's love of wood, nature, and music.

Mom was also creative, loved to sew, and taught all five of us girls to make our own clothes. She knitted, crocheted, did beautiful embroidery, and cooked incredible meals. She collected and often read to us the great books of art, music, and literature, which she bought on the installment plan at the local grocery store or through the mail. She would never allow us to complain that we were "bored" but insisted that we find creative things to do, and we did! Mom also fostered a great love of wildlife in me with frequent trips to the Mohegan Park Zoo in Norwich, which was filled with deer, owls, hawks, and even a monkey house.

Our local public high school, Norwich Free Academy, housed the fabulous Slater Museum and Art School, and I am so thankful to Mom for driving me there every Saturday morning throughout my elementary school years for drawing, painting, and pottery classes. We didn't have computers or video games—just an old black and white TV, so I had plenty of time to climb the big pine trees in our yard, sew, explore nature, read, play the piano, ride my bike, roller skate, paint and draw, and dream. I am so grateful for the wonderful childhood that I had. I know I would not be an artist today if it were not for those cherished years.

I attended the University of Connecticut as an art major and met my husband, Joe, there in 1971. We lived in Massachusetts for many years, and I received my B.A. degree and teaching certification in elementary education and art education from the University of Massachusetts. In 1981, we moved to Virginia. Joe and I live in a cozy old house in Hanover, Virginia, and have raised three wonderful daughters: Rachel, Rebecca, and Laura. We now share our home with our two dogs, Corky and Snow Bear. I have worn many artistic hats over the years, having worked as an elementary school teacher, art teacher, portrait artist at shopping malls and art shows, and scrimshaw artist, carving intricate designs into whalebone and elephant ivory. I've also worked as a landscape artist, working in oils, pastels, pen & ink, and pencil. For the past twenty years, I have taught piano and art lessons in my own home studio, the Harvest Moon Studio.

When I discovered pyrography in 2002, my life as an artist completely changed. I was deeply attracted to this craft because I have always had a deep love of nature and trees, and I just fell in love with the unique medium of drawing on wood. With each picture I complete, I see the potential for so many new effects and can't wait to try them out. I have met many interesting, creative, and talented people as I have explored this fascinating craft. After almost four years of studying and experimenting on my own, I took a class in woodburning with Orchid Davis at the John C. Campbell Folk School, in Brasstown, North Carolina. Orchid's excellent instruction and encouragement were invaluable to me, and I was very honored to be asked by her to teach woodburning classes at the school, which I began to do in August 2009.

Exploring the craft of woodburning has opened up my life in so many new and exciting ways. I hope it will do the same for you!

CONTENTS

ABOUT THIS BOOK

Whether you're a beginner, intermediate, or advanced woodburning enthusiast, this book covers everything from basic burning tools, how to transfer a pattern, easy burning and coloring techniques, shading and texturing techniques, and how to sand and finish your pieces. The projects range from basic to advanced. They teach you how to create your own unique patterns by choosing a central image, some border accents, and even a favorite saying to personalize the work. By choosing individual design elements and combining them with the mix-and-match pattern section of the book, even the simplest woodburned designs can create subtle and rich effects. From the smallest keychain to a framed wall hanging, the possibilities are limitless!

The "Crazy Quilt Sampler" practice project. Chapter 2 teaches the capabilities of various woodburning tips and helps you build a vocabulary of textures that you can use in your woodburnings (see page 26).

The "Saw-Whet Owl" is the book's main step-by-step project. It begins in chapter 4 (page 66).

You learn how to transfer the pattern from paper to wood.

Easy-to-follow directions guide you through the steps for completing the central image, the border, and even adding an optional saying or poem to make the woodburning even more distinctive.

INTRODUCTION

More and more people are beginning to rediscover the deep satisfaction and peace that can be found in the creative arts.

As a teacher, I believe that woodburning is a craft that is accessible to everyone, and there is no need of formal art training. Happily, woodburning is an art form that requires minimal workspace and doesn't create a big mess in your home. It is easy to learn, fun, and rewarding, and you will be amazed at how rapidly your abilities grow and improve with just a small investment of time, patience, and practice. Best of all, you don't need to know how to draw to get started with this book! Woodburning is not an expensive craft either; a high-quality burner, a few tips, and wooden objects to woodburn can be obtained easily and at minimal cost.

I discovered woodburning at a craft show in 2002, when I saw a portrait of an Indian chief burned into a basswood plaque. I was immediately intrigued and fascinated by the sepia-toned, engraved-looking burned lines, contrasting with the warm, natural wood tones and grain of the wood. I had worked with many painting and drawing media, and done scrimshaw, but had never seen anything quite as unique and beautiful as this.

I have always loved to draw, and I immersed myself with sheer delight in the study of pyrography, experimenting with different woodburners, tips, types of wood, and staining and finishing techniques. I learned the primary importance of including fun and love in the preparation and completion of a woodburning, and I found that the pieces that satisfied me the most came from my heart. Of course, I also made mistakes as I was learning these new skills by trial and error, and you can reap the benefit of my struggles by learning some very easy ways

to fix common mishaps. You will find that wood is actually a surprisingly forgiving medium.

This is a book for beginners, intermediates, and advanced woodburning enthusiasts. I show you how to find sources of inspiration and subject matter for pyrography, and I cover everything from basic burning tools, through how to transfer a pattern, easy burning and coloring techniques, shading and texturing techniques, and how to sand and finish your pieces. I have carefully designed the projects in this book for you, ranging from very basic to more advanced, so you can spend many quiet, peaceful hours experiencing the joy of pyrography while creating personalized gifts and unique accents for your home. You will be amazed at how even the simplest woodburned designs can create such subtle and rich effects!

Don't be concerned if you think you don't know how to draw. As you begin these projects, you can simply use the ready-made complete patterns provided for you, which can easily be transferred to the wood. As you become more confident, you can learn to create your own unique patterns that truly express your spirit by choosing individual design elements and combining them with the mix-and-match pattern section of the book. For example, you could begin with a central image, add a simple or more complex border to your design, and perhaps even add a poem or saying to personalize your work even more.

There are so many ways to use woodburning. A woodburned platter looks lovely as a wall hanging, and you can frame woodburnings done on birch panels. Woodturners can burn small vignettes and designs to accentuate their platters and bowls, using the grain of the wood as part of the design. Basket makers can use these designs on their woven baskets, and the patterns also work well for woodburning on gourds. Picture frames, mirror frames, box lids, chess or checker boards, wooden utensils, stepstools, and furniture can all be enhanced with woodburning designs. From the smallest keychain to a large, framed, woodburned wall hanging, the possibilities are limitless!

When exhibiting my work at craft shows, I have sometimes overheard a disconcerting comment from people looking at my woodburnings: "These are made by a laser— they aren't handmade." I suppose it *is* a sort of backhanded compliment to hear that my work looks that good! I can assure you that I have designed, hand-drawn, and hand-burned every line in these pieces and patterns, and now it gives me great fulfillment to share them with you. I hope they will provide you with many happy hours of creativity and results you can be proud of.

Well, enough talk! Let's turn up the heat, and start creating some woodburnings!

VARIATIONS ON A PATTERN

To give you an idea of how differently artists will interpret a theme, even when using the same patterns, study the student work presented at right. Three different moods and interpretations were created using the same lighthouse pattern. One student decided to create a simple border, while the others used only the central image pattern. You can see how unique and individual the results can be. It may inspire you to know that two of the students were beginners and had not tried woodburning until this class!

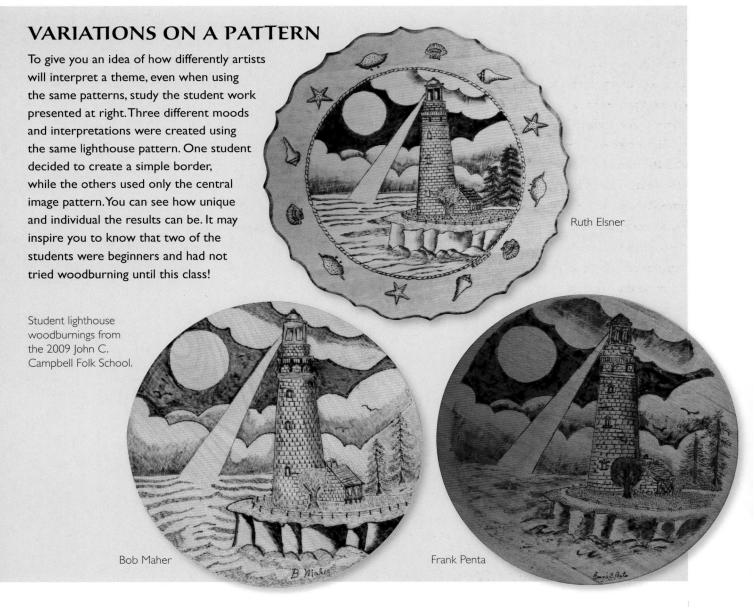

Ruth Elsner

Student lighthouse woodburnings from the 2009 John C. Campbell Folk School.

Bob Maher

B. Maher

Frank Penta

Chapter 1:
GETTING STARTED

   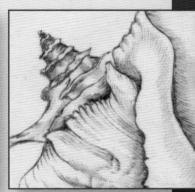

A piece of wood, a woodburning machine, a few simple supplies, and the desire to create a picture that excites you—that's all you need to get started! The simplicity of the tools and setup needed for woodburning makes it an ideal and affordable hobby.

TOOLS AND MATERIALS

Every teacher has a different way of doing things, uses different techniques and materials, and achieves widely varying effects. I share with you the materials and techniques that have worked for me. You will also benefit from studying other teachers' books to broaden your appreciation of the incredible potential of the art of pyrography.

SELECTING A WOODBURNING MACHINE

Choosing a pyrography machine is a personal decision that can be bewildering because there are so many types and brands of woodburners available, each claiming to be the best! I'll discuss the advantages and disadvantages of three types of woodburners I have used. I now work with the Colwood Detailer, exclusively.

It is worth investing in the best materials you can afford. As with most projects, your tools have a great effect on your level of achievement and the quality of your work, and thus, your satisfaction with it. In this book, you discover which tools best suit your needs as you experiment with the projects.

If your budget is a major factor, you can start with a simpler and less expensive woodburner (as I did in the beginning), but do not blame yourself if you are unable to achieve lifelike detail. I do not want you to be discouraged by the limitations of inexpensive tools.

Basic, one-temperature "soldering iron" type woodburner. Many people have had great success with this inexpensive tool. I used it for my first year learning pyrography, mainly because I didn't know that variable temperature woodburners existed. It is readily available at local arts-and-crafts stores. The tool heats to a pre-set, high-heat, temperature and uses solid brass, interchangeable burning tips that screw on to the tool head. There are several tip styles

available: a universal tip, used for fine-line and shading work; a calligraphy tip, used for lettering; a flow tip, used to fill in large areas; and a cone tip, which creates fine detailing. There is also a large shading tip available, which burns large areas and shadows.

The disadvantages of this type of tool include limitations in achieving lifelike detail without scorching or burning the wood. I would accidentally create holes in the wood that could not be scraped away. I found it difficult to control because I could not adjust the heat settings and the tool became very hot while I worked. Also, it was necessary to wait for the tip to cool down before I could change tips.

Nevertheless, some crafters love this tool and have great success with it, so I don't want to malign it. To each his own, as the saying goes. Although I rapidly became frustrated with this tool, I was forced to continue using it until a friend mentioned that a Woodcraft store in Richmond had variable-temperature pyrography machines. I was thrilled, and drove down to investigate right away.

The hot-wire pyrography machine. The British Janik is a European-style burner with a variable temperature control. It doesn't have a solid working point but uses a flexible point, or nib, that is made from a short length of nickel chromium wire. There is a power box with an on/off switch, and a dial that allows you to change the temperature of the nib. The nibs are changed by loosening the two connection screws, swapping the nib for a new, handmade one, and retightening. The wire point can be shaped into a spoon point, or other shapes, by hammering out the wire into flat shapes.

Because I am not especially mechanically gifted, a disadvantage for me was that it was time consuming to make the new tips by hand, and I wasn't able to make good ones

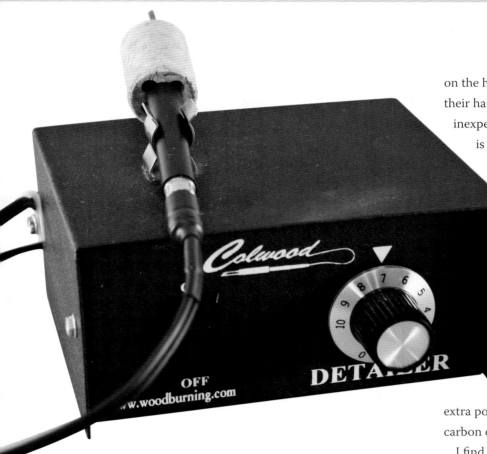

Colwood Detailer Woodburner with heavy-duty, 16-gauge cord.

on the handle. For those who have arthritis in their hands or fingers, as I do, I recommend the inexpensive custom cork heat shield, which is almost 1 inch (25mm) in diameter, and ¼ inch (6mm) thick. You can remove the thinner cork grips that come with the fixed tips and replace them with the custom cork heat shields. I have extra-thick custom cork heat shields on all of my hand pieces, and I am able to burn comfortably, even at high heat settings, for hours.

Colwood now offers all of their tips with extra burnishing or polishing for a small charge. The extra polishing helps to prevent the build-up of carbon on the tips.

I find that I am able to do all of my pyrography work with only five fixed tips. The following tips are the ones I recommend, and I will give a brief overview of what they can be used for. (A much more detailed discussion of the capabilities of each of these tips will be found in Chapter 2, as we work through the Crazy Quilt Sampler Project, which is a Practice Burning exercise).

Of course, there is an array of other tips available that you might like to try, but these five are all you need to create an infinite variety of lines and textures. They are definitely all you need to do every project in this book.

Some of you may already have different brands of woodburners or tips from another maker. Just compare the tips that you currently have with the pictures here, or on the Colwood Web site, *www.woodburning.com*, to see if they are similar. Also, many of the Colwood fixed tips can be used with other brands of woodburning machines, although sometimes a special adapter may be needed.

consistently. Also, I had to buy an expensive electrical adapter to use the unit in the United States.

The Colwood Detailer woodburner. This woodburner is a high-quality, affordably priced, variable temperature machine that can be adjusted at the base thermostat for a range of temperatures. Nibs become hot within seconds, and the cool down time is also fast. It is available with either interchangeable tips, or permanent, fixed tips, each with its own handle. I prefer the fixed tips because I don't have to wait for the tips to cool down before changing them. I have found that the fixed tips are sturdy and last a long time; I'm still using the same ones after four years! Be sure to get the heavy-duty 16-gauge cord.

Five recommended tips. The Colwood line of fixed tips comes with hand pieces made from a nonmetallic material that keeps them from becoming uncomfortably hot to handle. Each hand piece comes with its own cork grip

One of my favorite tips is the **Tight Round tip** (**1**). This versatile tip can be used for almost anything, from fur to feathers as well as an infinite variety of shading strokes. It turns on a curve in a tight radius because the tip is rounded and can make beautiful curved lines. It can also be laid flat on its side and used for shading smaller areas or on its edge to make straight lines. Colwood offers the **J tip** in its catalog and online, but you can call Colwood to special order the **Mini J**, which is smaller than the regular J, at no extra cost. I prefer the Mini J to the J because I do highly detailed work and can make much smaller curves with the Mini J.

Another of my favorite tips is the **Small Calligraphy tip** (**2**). I find it indispensable because it's really three tips in one. When using the corner of the tip, it performs like the C writing tip. When held horizontally on the burning surface, it can be used as a shading tip, and when held at a 45° angle, it can be used as a calligraphy tip.

The S tip, also known as the **Shading tip** (**3**), is wonderful for shading large areas. It is capable of making dark textured shading or light and subtle burnished effects that create the illusion of burled wood on a piece of plain wood.

The C tip is also known as the **Writing tip** (**4**) and glides on the wood just like a ballpoint pen. It is great for fine details.

The **Micro C tip** (**5**) is wonderful for extremely fine writing, shading, and tiny details, and for signing your name.

Some woodburning enthusiasts enjoy doing very precise architectural work or nature studies that require extreme detail or straight lines. For these readers, I recommend two additional Colwood tips. The first is the **Needle Point tip**, which is similar to a sewing

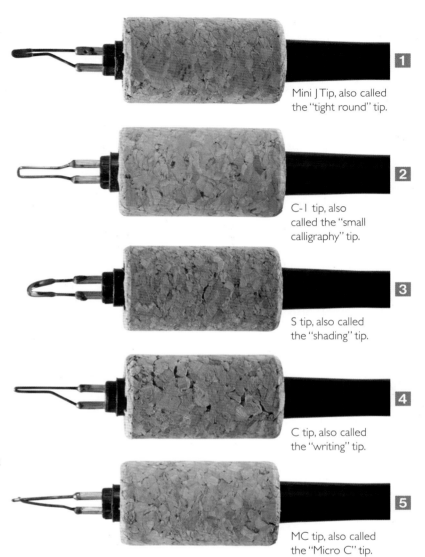

1 Mini J Tip, also called the "tight round" tip.

2 C-1 tip, also called the "small calligraphy" tip.

3 S tip, also called the "shading" tip.

4 C tip, also called the "writing" tip.

5 MC tip, also called the "Micro C" tip.

needle and is useful for extremely fine details, or delicate pointillistic stippling that even the Micro C cannot equal. The second additional tip I would recommend is the **MR Rounded Heel tip**, often referred to as a "skew" because it comes to a point. The heel on this tip has been rounded off, to prevent digging into the wood.

GOOD WOODS TO USE

There are many types of wood that are suitable for woodburning; but in general, the softer, evenly textured woods are easier and more consistent to burn on, especially for the beginning pyrographer. Light-colored wood allows for the best contrast between the burned lines and the surface. Also, it helps to have as little grain as possible, to provide a sort of blank canvas.

All of the projects in this book were done on basswood and birch, and these are the two types of wood I highly recommend for the beginning pyrographer. There are many wonderful books on pyrography that discuss the qualities of every type of wood species available and the advantages and disadvantages of each in terms of woodburning, coloring, and finishing. As you progress in your study of woodburning and become more confident, you can experiment with darker or more heavily grained woods, which can be an interesting challenge, because the grain of the wood can be incorporated into the design with beautiful and dramatic results.

Woodturners have a great advantage in being able to create their own beautiful, hand-turned platters made out of gorgeous wood like cedar, cherry, or maple. The grain lines and knots in these platters can suggest unique and lovely compositions.

Basswood. Basswood comes from the linden tree, and although it is listed as a hardwood species, it is actually a very soft wood with a lovely, warm, creamy color. The pale color and even grain provide an ideal surface for woodburning because the burned lines contrast vividly with the light color of the wood. It is readily available and can be purchased inexpensively at local arts and crafts stores in many shapes and sizes, such as bark-edged plaques, plates, boxes, or frames. The unfinished wood products company Walnut Hollow makes many lovely basswood shapes that can be woodburned.

You will find a great selection of wood supply companies on the Internet. Beautifully made, finely sanded, hand-turned basswood plates can be purchased from specialty shops such as Unique Woods. You can view their line of wood products at *www.uniquewoods.com*. Basswood plates come in many styles, with plain or scalloped edges, and flat, beaded, or beveled surfaces. If it is available, I always request the clear plate upgrade, which means the supplier will select the pieces with the least amount of grain or knots. Basswood plates come pre-sanded to a beautiful finish; there is usually no need for further sanding before woodburning. All of the projects in this book on rounded platters were done on the beautiful handturned basswood plates from Montzka Woodworking, based in Forest Lake, Minnesota (*tpmontzka@aol.com*). Montzka Platters are available retail through Unique Woods.

Baltic birch plywood panels. White birch has an extremely pale, cream color, which makes it ideal for showing off complex shading and line. There is sometimes more grain to deal with than in basswood, but it is still easily workable. It is available at Woodcraft or wood specialty stores, where they will often cut it for you to your desired sizes. Plywood panels are available in Baltic birch, which is very inexpensive, or in Finland birch, which has risen to quite a high price in recent years. I find that the Baltic birch is perfectly adequate. The panels come in a variety of thicknesses, from 1/16-inch (2mm) veneer to 5/8-inch (15mm) thick plywood. I use the 1/4-inch (6mm) thick panels, which can be easily framed. Be sure to store them flat so that they don't warp. I frame each finished piece, not only to give it the finishing touch but to prevent warping.

This is a good spot to discuss the use of pine wood for woodburning. At local craft shops, you can find many intriguing, unfinished plaques, shelves, boxes, clocks, and so forth made of pine. Although pine is definitely not my first choice of wood for woodburning, you can create lovely woodburned designs on these inexpensive pieces. Just be aware that pine is a soft wood and can have strong grain lines, knots, and imperfections that you will need to work with! As a beginner, you will be much better off to learn how to use your tips on basswood or birch, which have a much more even grain.

WOOD PREPARATION

Hand sanding. When I first began doing woodburnings, I simply hand-sanded my piece of wood, all in one direction, with a piece of 220- to 250-grit sandpaper. I then dusted the piece off with a soft lint-free cloth and was ready to go. I was quite satisfied with this minimalist approach for seven years, not knowing any better. Many woodburning enthusiasts are perfectly happy with this approach, and you may be as well. You can certainly do all of the projects in this book using this simple and inexpensive method, but please read the section on Machine Sanding before making your decision.

To hand sand, fold the sandpaper once or twice to make it easier to grip and sand with strokes in the direction of the wood grain using just the weight of your hand. Sanding against the grain will roughen the surface. Try to run the sandpaper along the full length of the wood with each stroke. I like to sand outdoors, away from my woodburning work area, because a lot of dust can be created. Use a lint-free cloth to dust off the wood, and you're ready to transfer your design.

Machine sanding. When I was introduced to the random orbit sander, it was love at first sight, and now I can't live without it! I couldn't believe the difference it made to do woodburning on a polished, highly sanded surface. The tip just glides, and I have so much more control over the lines because the tips do not catch so easily in the burnished wood grain. I have also found that pre-sanding favorably affects the application of color, whether watercolors or oil paints, as well as how well the final finish takes.

The random orbit sander is my tool of choice. But be sure and shop around for tools that are right for you. To me, it's worth it to invest a little more in my woodburning craft. This sander is small, light-weight, and easy to use, even for the power-tool phobic. I use a sander with Velcro hook-and-loop sandpaper discs, not PSA glue-on discs. I can re-use the sandpaper discs, and they

The Random Orbit Sander is small, light-weight, and easy to use. I recommend a sander that uses Velcro-type hook and loop sandpaper discs.

last a long time! Mine is a Porter Cable Random Orbit Sander, Model 343. It uses inexpensive 5" (127mm) sanding discs with eight holes each. The discs easily attach to the sander with the Velcro hook and loop.

I place a piece of inexpensive, bumpy-textured, plastic shelving cloth (easily found in the kitchen department) under the wood to hold it in place as I sand. Remember—the higher the number of the sandpaper, the finer the grit. You don't want to start off sanding with a higher, finer grit—begin sanding with *coarser* sandpaper first. For example, start with a 120-grit pad, then switch to 220, and then 320. If the wood is relatively smooth to begin with, and you are not trying to erase mars or marks, you would start with the 220-grit pad. You can go all the way up to a 600-grit pad or even higher, if you desire. I find I am usually satisfied with 320-grit sanding.

Don't press too hard. Let the weight of the machine do the work for you. Gentle pressure is all you need. You can even create an attractive beveled effect on the edges of your piece with your sander. I also occasionally use the sander to erase major mistakes. Great care must be taken in doing this, and I resort to this method only in dire emergencies! (You will find more information on easy ways to remedy mistakes in Chapter 3).

After sanding, dust off your piece with a lint-free cloth, and you're ready to transfer your pattern.

PATTERN TRANSFER SUPPLIES

To create and transfer designs and patterns, you will need **high-transparency tracing paper**, and **wax-free graphite transfer paper**. Saral is an excellent brand. It is very important that you do not use ordinary carbon paper, which makes lines that will not erase from the wood.

Many people like to use a red ballpoint pen when transferring a design so that they can see which portions have been done. Soft artist kneaded erasers can be used to blot up excess graphite after the transfer is complete.

MISCELLANEOUS SUPPLIES

Small "snap-off" utility knife for scraping out highlights in dark areas and fixing mistakes.

Masking tape, transparent tape.

Paper towels for blotting watercolors and stain.

Straight-edge and curved **rulers and protractors**, and **circle, rectangle, and square templates**. I love to collect odd rulers and templates with interesting shapes to use in designs. My favorite is a flexible ruler that I can use to create circles, ovals, and free-form curves, which is especially handy when designing borders.

Soft pencils (2B or 4B) for drawing on the wood surface. Marks from soft pencils are more easily erased or sanded away. Hard pencils can leave indentations in the wood that will affect the smooth glide of your woodburning tips.

Miscellaneous supplies include pencils, tape, rulers, erasers, nail files, and tracing paper.

Pencil sharpener. I love my electric pencil sharpener. However, I have also become a big fan of the inexpensive Papermate Sharpwriter mechanical pencils.

Erasers. I prefer the soft, grey artists' kneaded erasers, which do not leave marks on the wood.

A fabulous tool if used properly, the kneaded eraser is meant to be molded, pinched, and kneaded in your hands, just like Silly Putty! It can be stretched out and reformed into a ball, to clean it. If the eraser is not kneaded and "warmed up" before using, it won't work much better than an ordinary eraser. When properly kneaded before using it each time, you will find that it gently cleans up smudges and lightens and erases transfer lines on the wood with amazing efficiency. It is also therapeutic, kind of like a "worry stone."

Scrap pieces of birch or basswood on which to practice strokes.

Nail files for cleaning carbon build-up off tips. I like the type of nail file with 220 grit on one side and 320 on the other side. (More information on keeping tips clean is found in Practice Projects in Chapter 2).

Lint-free cloths to dust off woodburnings. Lint-free cloth looks like T-shirt material and can be purchased inexpensively by the bagful in the paint department of any hardware store.

Kneaded eraser, warmed up and stretched out.

Optional: Recorded books on tape or CD to listen to while burning. I find having my mind pleasantly occupied really helps the work to flow. I also find that long telephone conversations are a great time for woodburning—I can occupy my hands and create something beautiful while I catch up with friends.

COLORING SUPPLIES NEEDED FOR THE PROJECTS IN THIS BOOK

I prefer to use coloring techniques in which the paint remains transparent and the woodburned lines show clearly through the glaze of color. My two favorite media for coloring my woodburnings are: oil paints thinned to transparency with low-odor mineral spirits; and color washes with watercolor paints. In this book, all of the projects that require coloring can be done with watercolors. Many pyrographic artists also have great success in coloring their work with colored pencils, acrylics, gouache, fabric dyes, translucent acrylic inks, metallic paints, or even nail polish. (More information on coloring techniques will be found in the Practice Projects section of Chapter 3 on page 64).

Watercolor paints. To assure lightfastness and vibrancy of color, always buy the highest quality professional paints you can afford. I use Winsor and Newton Professional Artists' Water Colours, or Daniel Smith Watercolors. For the Crazy Quilt Sampler practice project, and for most of the other projects in the book, you will need the following colors: yellow ochre light, brown ochre, raw sienna, burnt sienna, quinacrodone gold, Van Dyke brown, burnt umber, raw umber.

As you work your way through the projects and develop your woodburning skills, you

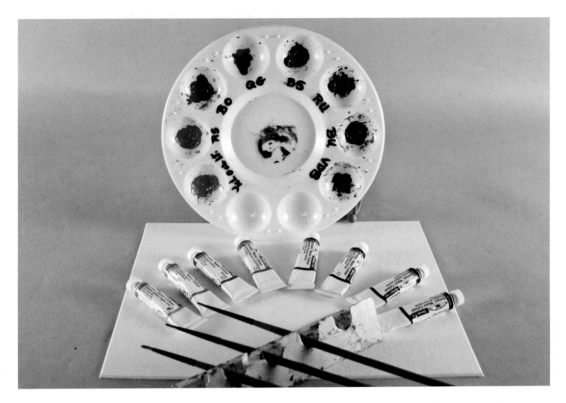

Coloring supplies.
Always buy the highest quality professional paints you can afford.

will probably want to add other colors to your collection. But these will make a fine beginning.

Brushes. All you need are a few inexpensive, soft bristle, synthetic or sable brushes that come to a point (rounds). Good sizes are 2, 4, 6, and 8.

Mixing tray. Inexpensive white plastic trays with many shallow wells and mixing areas are readily available at craft shops.

FINAL FINISHING SUPPLIES

People seem to have a natural desire to touch woodburnings! They love to feel the textured lines, and stroke the wood. It's important to provide protection to your finished pieces, and to guard against the effects of direct sunlight as well. Sunlight can, over time, darken the surface of the wood, and affect the density of finely burned lines.

My own experience with finishing has been experimental. I make no claim to being an expert on stains, sealers, varnishes, polyurethane products, or oil or acrylic coatings. These products can produce unpredictable effects on different types of wood. However, I will share with you what has worked for me.

Spray-on finishes. For those who prefer the ease of using a spray, there are many brands of spray-on polyurethane, such as Krylon, in matte or glossy finishes. Apply half a dozen very light coats, waiting 30 minutes between each coat. I use this method most of the time. I wait until I am absolutely certain I am finished with the piece because woodburning through varnish releases toxic fumes.

Rub-on finish. I am pleased to share with you a finishing technique that uses a homemade combination of ingredients called the thirds mixture (see sidebar, page 22). The method is easy, and the results are consistently beautiful.

THIRDS MIXTURE

In a clean jar, mix together:

- 1/3 Clear oil polyurethane (do not use the water-based variety), available at Lowe's or Home Depot—either gloss or satin is fine. (If you use the satin, be sure to stir or shake it up first.) The polyurethane acts as the drier in this mixture.

- 1/3 Mineral spirits—I use the low-odor variety, also available at Lowe's or Home Depot.

- 1/3 100% Pure tung oil—(Be sure to get pure tung oil, not tung oil finish). This product is available at Woodcraft stores or through wood product catalogs.

I recommend stirring the mixture with a wooden paint stick before using it each time, since the mixture can separate.

I use a glass jar with a screw-on cap and find that placing a piece of aluminum foil under the cap can help to prevent the lid from sticking to the jar. To protect my hands, I always wear the blue-colored nitrile gloves, which do not allow solvents to penetrate, because I am susceptible to headaches from solvents. Also, because my woodburning studio is in the central part of my home, I do all my finishing outdoors, to keep my home free of toxic fumes.

First, carefully remove any pencil marks or smudges from your woodburning. Apply the thirds mixture to the wood surface with a paper towel, stroking in the direction of the grain. Unlike a lacquer, the mixture will penetrate and soak into the wood surface. It doesn't take much to create a light coat, so it is important to only use very small amounts of the mixture and to continually wipe away excess mixture with a clean paper towel. Do be careful that you don't leave any puddled residue on the wood or let the mixture just sit on the surface; it will crystallize and could ruin the surface.

One light coat will provide enough protection to the wood, but if you prefer a slightly darker color, you can apply a second coat. Allow each coat to sit overnight before applying the next coat. After the final coat, let the piece dry for several days. You can apply as many coats as you like, but I often stop with just one coat, which provides enough protection. You can even touch up the varnish coating on your woodburning years later with another coat of this mixture.

Tip: In many of my designs, I have areas I prefer to keep light-colored, such as the moon, or areas of wood directly underneath lettering. I apply the thirds mixture with only one extremely light coat to these lightest areas and put more coats on the areas I prefer a little darker. You can try the finish on a scrap piece of wood first to see how it will look. On areas I want to be extremely light, I may not put any thirds mixture at all and simply leave the wood bare.

Because all of the projects in this book can be done with basswood or birch, you should not have any problem applying this finish to these woods. But other woods will react differently to this mixture. Some woods, such as cedar, will require more mixture to be applied because it will soak in deeply. Cherry wood may "bleed" out a reddish color—simply wipe off and reapply the mixture.

FOR A HARDER FINISH

For some projects, such as a checkerboard or lazy Susan, you may prefer a harder finish to protect the wood surface. To create a harder surface, after applying your first coat as detailed above, you can apply the following mixture as your final coat (usually the second coat). Notice there is no tung oil in this mixture.

- 2/3 Clear oil polyurethane (gloss or satin).

- 1/3 Mineral spirits.

Apply and wipe off the excess, and allow to dry for a couple of days.

Note: I am grateful to Frank Penta, a highly respected woodturning teacher at the John C. Campbell Folk School, for sharing this wood finishing formula with me.

SETTING UP A COMFORTABLE WORKSPACE

A great advantage woodburners have over crafts people who do woodturning or woodworking is we are not weighed down with a lot of large, heavy, dust-generating equipment. Happily, woodburning is a craft that requires minimal workspace.

If it is possible for you to create a permanent workspace for yourself, it is such a joy to always have everything set up and waiting for you at a moment's notice. Here are some suggestions for creating a welcoming and efficient workspace that really does not require a lot of room.

Worktable. Some people prefer to work at a tilted drafting table, which I tried for many years. The disadvantage for me was not being able to spread my reference materials out around me. I like to work with leaves, shells, books, photos, etc., arranged nearby.

I now prefer to work at a flat table, but tilt my work up at an angle, with a book or two propped underneath. By tilting your work up, you can keep your head back as you work, which not only prevents neck and back strain, but also helps you to avoid breathing any smoke. On the flat table, I can surround myself with inspiration, and not worry about taping it to the sloped drafting table.

Lighting. To prevent eye strain and more easily appreciate the engraved textures you are creating on the wood surface, it helps to have really good lighting.

I use two angled swing-arm work lamps. The ones on the right and on the left are

My work area, with lights and fan. Tilting your work up helps you avoid breathing in smoke.

inexpensive lamps that clamp easily onto the table, can be moved in any direction, and use ordinary, 75-100 watt household bulbs. They are available at hardware stores or through art supply catalogs. This is all you really need to begin woodburning. Working with the lamp set at a slight angle to the surface of your woodburning will highlight the tiny shadows formed in the grooves and help you see how deeply you are burning.

Illuminated magnifier lamp. I recently purchased an illuminated magnifier lamp with a 6" (152mm) glass lens, 1.5x magnification, and a 30-watt circline fluorescent bulb. Because I like to do highly detailed work, I find this moderately priced lamp a joy to work with. I now highly recommend using a lighted magnifier lamp if you decide to invest a bit more in your woodburning hobby and enjoy doing finely detailed work. I find I do not hunch over when I work with this lamp, which helps a lot with back strain when working for long periods.

Also, I have found that working with magnification has improved the quality of my work, because if the details look good at high magnification, they will definitely look good to the naked eye!

Ventilation. It is important to work in a well-ventilated space when doing woodburnings. Most woodburning techniques will create little smoke, but if you burn for long periods at higher settings, as I often do, there is no denying that smoke can be a nuisance. To avoid sore throats or headaches from breathing smoke while you work, tilt your work and use a fan. I always work next to a window, and position the fan so that it sucks the smoke away from my hand and out the window. You don't want to have the fan blowing toward your work, because the air movement will cool the burning tip and make your burning inconsistent or ineffective.

In very cold or very hot weather, when opening the window is not an option, I am forced to simply have the fan blow the smoke away from me. On the plus side, woodburning will make the house smell delightfully cozy!

WORKING OUTDOORS FROM LIFE

Sometimes I like to set up out in the yard to draw and woodburn a particularly intriguing tree or branch from life. You will need a TV tray, a comfortable stool, a long, heavy-duty extension cord, a drawing board to rest your wood on, a few pencils and an eraser to

Outdoor woodburning set-up. You will need a TV tray, a comfortable stool, a long, heavy-duty extension cord, a drawing board to rest your wood on, a few pencils, and an eraser.

lightly indicate your composition, and you've got a unique way to enjoy nature while you sketch with your woodburner! (Please note that using too many lightweight extension cords connected to your burner can affect the consistency of heat levels as you work.)

WOODBURNING SAFETY

- Keep your work area neat and orderly.
- Be careful not to accidentally burn the wire coming from the machine.
- Rest your burning pen in the clip holder on top of the unit when not in use, not on your work.
- Always turn your burner off when not working or when changing tips.
- Do not leave children unsupervised near woodburning equipment.
- Never use a burner around combustible fuels or gases or near water.
- Don't open the case of the power unit of your woodburner; live terminals are exposed inside.

Especially important. Avoid burning any wood that has been pretreated with preservatives, such as pressure-treated lumber. These preservatives are toxic, and fumes can be released into the air as you work. Also avoid burning any wood that has been varnished, lacquered, painted, or sealed in any way, to avoid the release of toxic fumes. Never use medium-density fiberboard (MDF), cork, or other bonded material for pyrography because they can be made of toxic materials that when burned produce dangerous fumes harmful to your health.

Chapter 2:
DESIGN

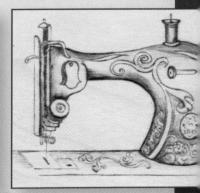

In my woodburning classes I have found that many otherwise highly skilled craftspeople have not had the opportunity to learn the basic concepts of creating realistic drawings. You will find it so much easier to create beautifully shaded and textured woodburnings if you understand some simple drawing concepts.

In Chapter 3, we do two practice woodburning projects that put these concepts to use. I know you are eager to begin woodburning, but it will be very helpful to take just a few minutes to study the following pages before beginning your first project.

BASIC DRAWING CONCEPTS USEFUL FOR WOODBURNERS

STEP 1: OUTLINES AND SHAPES

An area that is completely surrounded by lines becomes a shape. **The four basic shapes** are the circle, square, triangle, and free-form or organic shapes.

When these shapes, which are sometimes called forms, become truly three-dimensional (with an indication of height, width, depth, or thickness), they are named the sphere, cube, cone, and cylinder. Almost all objects in nature are composed of combinations of these four simple shapes, and it will help you in your drawings to see these shapes in the objects around you. For example, a tree trunk is an elongated cylinder, and a beach ball is a sphere.

Of course, you can easily see that you will seldom find perfectly symmetrical forms in nature. Most of the time, they are charmingly lopsided, bent, or distorted, and it is these very variations and peculiarities that make them interesting. Many artists love to draw dilapidated old barns and rusted, decrepit mailboxes for this very reason. Look for the unique features in the objects you choose to draw and woodburn, and emphasize them to keep your work from looking too stiff or mechanical.

STEP 2: CREATE SHAPES WITH BASIC TONE

Tone is simply the main overall lightness or darkness of an object and is usually referred to as value. You can see in the following value scale that values can range from very light, to medium, to extremely dark tones. Tone and color are not the same thing. A color can be very light or very dark in tone.

The Simple Value Scale, drawn in graphite. Light highlights and dark areas in your drawings give your work richness and depth.

In order to create a three-dimensional effect in your drawings and woodburnings, it is important to use the full range of light and dark values. You can create dramatic effects by using **value contrast**, which simply means being sure to have very light highlights *and* extremely dark areas in your drawings. This will give your work richness and depth.

In order to achieve strong value contrast, it is important to have the light coming from only one direction in your drawing or woodburning. Having many lights coming from many different angles will wash out and flatten the object, because there will be no definite place to put the shading. A basic rule of thumb to remember, in drawing, is to *light your drawing from one direction only*.

When I added the overall tone, or value, to the four basic shapes, it was important to first

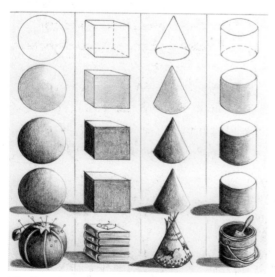

The Four Basic Shapes Drawing Chart, based on drawing principles taught by the great artist and teacher John Gnagy in the 1950s.

ask a fundamental question: "Which direction is the light coming from?" I decided that for the four basic shapes chart, I would have the light come from the upper right. This meant I needed to leave a white highlight on the top and right edge of each form. So the circle, for example, becomes a ball because of the illusion of three dimensions created by the highlight and tone.

STEP 3: ACCENTUATE THE SHAPE WITH SHADING

Shading is truly a magical ingredient in creating a realistic drawing or woodburning. It creates the illusion of three dimensions on the flat surface of your paper or piece of wood. Shading takes the value contrasts from the previous step beyond just the basic tone. When light shines on one side of an object, the other side becomes dark. So when you strive to represent a form in a drawing or a woodburning, you put your darkest shading on the darker side, and put the lightest tones and highlights on the parts of the object where the light hits it.

You can easily create gorgeous, subtle shading effects with your five woodburning tips, and we will explore and practice these in the next chapter, as we woodburn the Crazy Quilt Sampler. You will learn to create shading with stippling (dots), cross-hatching, contour lines, parallel lines, short "fur" strokes, wavy and free-form lines, and random "scribble" lines. We will also practice creating a soft, "burled wood" antiqued shading effect that can be created with the S tip.

In Chapter 3, we'll see a woodburned value scale created with the five woodburning tips and the techniques mentioned above to create areas of dark and light shading and texture.

For now, just realize shading is that special touch you can add to a drawing or woodburning, to make the forms look real. Sometimes, when you sketch objects from nature, they will be lit unevenly. As the artist, you can decide the best angle for the light to bring out the form, and then put the deepest shading on the opposite side of the light.

On curved forms like the sphere, cone, and cylinder, it is also important that the transitions in shading from dark areas to light areas be done *gradually*. For example, on a curved surface, you don't want an abrupt transition from dark to light, and there should be no harsh outlines or striped effects between shaded areas. In the spheres on the far left and the center, the sudden changes from dark to light do not look realistic. Soften the edges between the dark and light areas and make the transitions gentle ones, as in the sphere on the right.

Hard edges and soft edges. You can blur and soften the lines and shading in some areas of your woodburnings, such as for backgrounds. In the areas you would like to

Smooth transitions in shading improve your work by creating varied effects.

 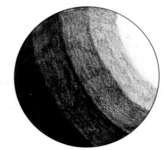 

focus attention on, use strong, crisp lines and more intense value contrasts. Using both hard and softened edges improves your work by creating varied effects.

> **TIP** An easy and effective trick is to darken and slightly thicken the outlines on the dark side of the object, and blend the outlines into the dark shading, to bring the drawing into sharper, more dramatic focus.

STEP 4: BE SURE TO INCLUDE SHADOWS CAST BY OBJECTS

Adding cast shadows will add even more realism to your woodburnings. When light shines on an object, the object casts a shadow onto another surface. Cast shadows create fascinating patterns that enhance and enliven your woodburning designs. Train your eyes to see the cast shadows of common things around you. For example, tree branches cast lovely, lacy shadow patterns on the light green grass of meadows or on a snow covered hillside.

Be careful not to make the cast shadow too thick or wide, or it will look like a paper cut-out, and appear to be standing up on its edge! Don't outline the cast shadow, but let the edges remain soft and blurred. When a cast shadow falls on an uneven surface, such as the shadow of a tree trunk falling on a rolling hillside, be

Realistic tree shadows. Cast shadows of a tree should "hug" the contours of the ground. (Detail from "Fragile Things.")

careful to make the shadow narrower than the trunk of the tree, and get even narrower as it moves away from the tree. The shadow should move with the shape of the hill, and appear to "hug the ground." Also, the cast shadow lightens and softens as it moves away from the tree. A straight, thick shadow will look primitive and amateurish. By giving careful thought to the underlying movement of the ground under the shadow, you learn to soften the shading so that it looks realistic.

STEP 5: TEXTURES ADD INTEREST

The Crazy Quilt Sampler Practice Project in Chapter 3 gives you ample opportunity to learn to create varied textures. With your woodburner and only five tips, you can easily create satisfying realism in your woodburnings by producing textures like smooth water ripples, roughened bricks, soft fur, fluffy feathers, or creviced tree bark. The weave of fabric or smooth gloss of an apple can be represented in a woodburning by patterns of lines, dots, or simply burnishing with a shading tip. Woodburned textures can be layered one over another to produce countless effects.

As you practice the line and shading techniques in this chapter, you'll find you can combine techniques to create tone, shading, shadows, and textures. Shading strokes can be done over stippling; crosshatching can be done over shading strokes, and so forth. Be aware there are an infinite number of ways to create effects of light and dark areas and the illusion of three dimensions. Through practice and experimentation, you gradually discover the effects that best express your personality and style.

SOURCES OF INSPIRATION

One of the most enjoyable tasks in designing a woodburning composition is the process of hunting for just the right reference material. I am continually on the lookout for new subjects that spark my imagination and resonate with a theme or poem I might have in mind.

It is helpful to create your own personal reference library of books that inspire you. These do not have to be expensive; I have found many treasured reference books at library used book sales, where I can fill an entire grocery bag with my finds for next to nothing! And don't forget to check out the children's book section at these sales; many books and magazines for children, such as *Ranger Rick* and *My Big Backyard*, are filled with wonderful photographs of animals, birds, and nature.

If you visit a botanical garden, be sure to look at the children's coloring book section. Many marvelous and inexpensive books contain line drawings of flowers, birds, insects, gardens, and trees that are ideal for woodburning.

It's also a good idea to keep a file of clip art. I have many shoeboxes filled with photographs and clipped pictures from magazines. There is no shortage of reference material, and if you collect, organize, and file it properly, you will have wonderful resources on hand for projects.

Although you certainly must respect copyrights, you can "paraphrase" other people's work with discretion by combining various images and altering them enough so that they are no longer recognizable as exact copies of original artwork. There are many places on the Internet, such as Google Images, or in art reference books where you can find copyright-free images. The library is one of my favorite resources for animal and nature reference material. You can find ideas in wallpaper pattern books and the designs on cloth at fabric stores. Many paint stores give out discontinued wallpaper books for free. Don't forget yard sales, and the book sections at Goodwill and the Salvation Army. Calendars

Sketchbook drawing of bluejays.

The "Simple Gifts" woodburning.

are also a fantastic resource for nature and wildlife photo reference. If your artwork is for personal enjoyment or created to give as gifts, and you appreciably alter or combine the photographic reference images you use, you do not need to be overly concerned about copyright law. But if you plan to sell or publish your artwork, be careful in your use of copyrighted materials.

For me, one of the very best sources of inspiration is Mother Nature herself. It is delightful to take a walk through my yard and carefully choose just the right leaf, branch, pine cone, or acorn to add to my composition. Sometimes I've even traced real leaves directly onto my pattern. No worries about copyright infringement there! I have a small collection of shells, bird nests, Indian corn, gourds, and other natural objects close by to inspire me. Many of my compositions have included dogwood leaves and blossoms, rosebuds, oak leaves, and winged seedpods picked from my garden. If you love birds, as I do, be sure to have several birdfeeders—mine are right outside our dining room window—and keep a camera handy!

If you are comfortable with drawing, please don't forget that old standby—the sketchbook. Sketching objects from nature or photographs helps develop an artist's eye for detail and the imagination to combine objects in a pleasing way.

TECHNOLOGY

Digital photography is a fantastic tool for the woodburning artist. I love not worrying about wasting film; I can simply delete the shots that are not successful.

One of the best investments of time and money is to take a beginner class in digital photography. I can now photograph my favorite subjects in botanical gardens, at the zoo, or at home. Best of all, I can immediately download the images onto my computer, then view, edit, and print them. The editing program Photoshop Elements is a simpler, user-friendly version of Photoshop. Images can easily be cropped, enlarged, reduced, converted to black and white, and printed. It's a wonderful way to turn your own photographs into black and white woodburning patterns.

I also use a scanner, which allows me to scan photographs and put them into a photo reference file on my computer. I can print them when I need them, in black and white, in the size I need.

If you are not comfortable using a computer, don't fret. For six years I did all my woodburning work without a digital camera or a computer to create patterns or print photographs. But now that I have made the leap, I enthusiastically recommend the computer as a tool if you are comfortable with technology.

SAYINGS

> Work is love made visible.
>
> Kahlil Gibran

In my artistic life, I find that including inspirational quotes and sayings in my artwork adds a deeper dimension.

Sometimes I find sayings or quotes that speak to me, and I create artwork inspired by them. Other times, I create a woodburning and then find a quote that enhances the image. Either way, as you can see from the woodburnings in this book, I personally love the magic that is created when art is combined with language. I have found great joy in being able to express myself creatively in this way, and I hope you do as well.

There are endless sources of inspiration for sayings you can use in your woodburnings. Excerpts from poetry, prose, and scripture, lyrics to songs or Broadway show tunes, hymns, nursery rhymes, favorite sayings—all of these can be included in your artistic creations. The Internet is also a fabulous resource.

HOW TO ADD A SAYING TO A CURVED OR CIRCULAR BORDER

It is easy to add lettering to a straight border. Adding a saying to a curved border is a bit more time consuming, although well worth the effort.

Simply print out your saying in the font and size you prefer. Draw ruled lines underneath and above the letters and cut them out in strips. Form the letters into curves by partially clipping the strip between words and letters, and then physically spread the paper apart between the letters to create the curved shape. The strip can now be taped to your pattern, or directly taped to the wood itself, and then transferred with graphite paper. Some very savvy computer whizzes are able to create curved words with just the right amount of curvature on the computer, but I find it much easier to do by hand.

Applying curved lettering. Here the curved lettering is taped in place and ready for transferring with graphite paper.

Of course, including sayings in your artwork is a personal choice. Below is an assortment of sayings that might spark some ideas for you. You can experiment with the size and placement of the letters, various font styles, and whether the saying looks better capitalized or not.

It is your composition, so get creative and have fun!

"Words are the voice of the heart."
—Confucius

"Language exerts hidden power, like the moon and the tides."
—Rita Mae Brown

"Poetry is when an emotion has found its thought and the thought has found words."
—Robert Frost

"Mothers hold their children's hands for a little while, but their hearts forever."
—Unknown

"Be the change you wish to see in the world."
—Gandhi

"Families are like fudge—mostly sweet with a few nuts."
—Unknown

"It is better to light one small candle than to curse the darkness."
—Eleanor Roosevelt

"Women are like teabags. We don't know our true strength until we are in hot water!"
—Eleanor Roosevelt

"I saw the angel in the marble and carved until I set him free."
—Michelangelo

"Imagination is more important than knowledge."
—Einstein

"Your vocation is the place where your deep gladness and the world's deep hunger meet."
—Frederick Buechner

"Blessed is the man who has found his work."
—Author Unknown

"Little ideas that tickle and nag and refuse to go away should never be ignored, for in them lie the seeds of destiny."
—Farmer Hoggert in the film Babe

"If one advances confidently in the direction of his dreams, and endeavors to live the life which he has imagined, he will meet with a success unexpected in common hours."
—Henry David Thoreau

"What lies behind us and what lies before us are tiny matters compared to what lies within us."
—Ralph Waldo Emerson

"Whatever you can do, or dream you can, begin it. Boldness has genius, power and magic in it."
—Goethe

"Ordinary riches can be stolen, real riches cannot. In your soul are infinitely precious things that cannot be taken from you."
—Oscar Wilde

"Dreams are illustrations ... from the book your soul is writing about you."
—Marsha Norman

"No act of kindness, however small, is ever wasted."
—Aesop, in The Lion and the Mouse

"The more I think about it, the more I realize there is nothing more artistic than to love others."
—Vincent Van Gogh

"Every day is a new beginning!"
—Author Unknown

"Every great dream begins with a dreamer."
—Harriet Tubman

"I do not want to die until I have faithfully made the most of my talent and cultivated the seed that was placed in me, until the last small twig has grown."
—Cathe Kollwitz

"Tall oaks from little acorns grow."
—Author Unknown

"What pleasant paths begin in gardens."
—Author Unknown

HOW A PATTERN COMES TOGETHER

A thing of beauty is a joy forever.
John Keats

BRIEF OVERVIEW

You can use the ready-made complete composition patterns provided for you in this book (see page 102) to build your confidence as a woodburner. Eventually, however, you will probably want to try your hand at designing your own compositions.

I have tried to simplify this process for you by providing a large number of patterns to choose from in the mix-and-match section of this book (see page 82).

For example, you could first choose a central image pattern from either the Complete Compositions, or the Elements section. If you want a border, you could decide which elements best complement the central image you have chosen and combine them in a pleasing way. You could choose the chipmunk for your central image, and then combine acorns and leaves in a complementary design in your border area. If you would like to add a saying to your composition, you can refer to the section on Sayings (page 33).

Let me walk you through a detailed explanation of the process of creating a woodburning design and pattern. Again, if you prefer, you can skip this section for now and simply use the ready-made patterns. After you have some experience with woodburning, please do return to this section. You'll be pleasantly surprised by how easily you can design your own patterns!

PLANNING YOUR COMPOSITIONS

In essence, composition is simply the arrangement of your subject matter within your picture space. The elements that make up a composition are color, value, lines, and textures, as well as the shapes and sizes of subjects, and whether they are primarily vertical, horizontal, or diagonal.

The most important thing is to lay out the elements (trees, animals, teapots, or other objects) so that there is a natural balance to the composition. Avoid clustering all the objects on one side or in one corner of the space. It is also important to have a pleasing balance of dark and light areas.

In some woodburnings, I will start with a poem or saying, and look for images to illustrate this theme. In others, I begin with a central image that appeals to me, and build on that. I find it deeply gratifying to play with words and images, and move them around in different arrangements until I feel they have a balance and harmony that satisfies me.

One of the best ways to try out your ideas is by doing quick "thumbnail sketches" to help you visualize how your subject will look in different formats. I find I have much more of a comfort level when I play with my woodburning compositions on paper first, rather than drawing directly on the wood. It is difficult to completely erase incorrect pencil

This composition was overdone and could have been much simpler. The woodburning became too dark with too few light areas of bare wood to balance the busy details. Sometimes "less is more," and in this piece, more was definitely less effective.

lines from the wood surface, and the pencil can leave unwanted indentations in the wood.

By taking the time to sketch carefully planned, well balanced, and pleasing compositions on paper first, you can create designs and patterns that you can then easily transfer to the wood. When you begin the actual woodburning, you will be much more confident if you have worked out the arrangement of forms and the spacing of words or border elements beforehand. This planning stage can take a long time, from hours to even days. I have learned to relax, be generous with myself, and take my time!

THOUGHTS ON THE CREATIVE PROCESS

Some woodburning designs come together quickly; one shape simply suggests another, and the composition develops with a gentle, instinctive flow of ideas. This is wonderful when it happens, but I often find that I seem to need to "percolate" ideas for a while, spending many happy hours looking at photographs and books and reading poetry. I used to feel impatient with this stage, worrying that I was just procrastinating, and that this was time wasted. But I've come to believe that giving myself permission to be in this percolating mode helps me to go deeper. Coming up with concepts, images and words that feel "just right" and that have profound meaning for me has become one of the most important and enjoyable aspects of designing my compositions. It is fun to find new ways of expressing myself—from whimsical and humorous ideas, to deeply inspirational, spiritual, or solemn thoughts and images.

BORDERS

First, let's talk about borders. The interplay of images and words, and the contrasts of pattern against pattern in a border design, create a beautiful visual frame for your central image and add deeper layers of meaning and interest to enhance your work.

Borders can be informal or ornate—from the simplest flowers in alternating patterns to the interlocking complexity of Celtic knot work designs, all the way to the awe-inspiring borders and scrollwork of medieval illuminated manuscripts. Designs can be stylized, geometric, abstract, symmetrical, or natural and free flowing—the sky's the limit!

By experimenting with as wide a range of ideas as possible, you will eventually develop an original style and unique visual vocabulary of your own. The more experienced you become, the more elaborate and distinctive the designs you will be capable of producing.

Take a few minutes to browse through the Elements pattern section of the book (page 82), to get ideas for motifs you might like to include in your border designs.

Autumn-themed border. Gourds, pumpkins, berries, and Indian corn can be combined into a seasonally themed border. (Detail from border of "I'll Put a Trinket On.")

Springtime border. Birds' nests and flying birds can be alternated to create a flowing springtime border. (Detail from border of "Simple Gifts.")

Sewing arts border. Sewing machines, thimbles, thread, tape measures, and buttons can be woven into a pattern that celebrates the fiber arts. Use items from any hobby to make an interesting and cohesive border. (Detail from "Young at Heart.")

Evergreen border. Pinecones and branches make a lovely, graceful frame for a central image. (Detail from "All Things Wise and Wonderful.")

Acorns and seedpods. A tapestry ribbon of acorns and winged seedpods provides a natural kind of feeling. You can walk outside any time of year and find an endless variety of leaf shapes, seedpods, delicate ferns, and catkins to use in this kind of border. (Detail from "Only God Can Make a Tree.")

CONTENTS OF A BORDER

Natural images can be used from nature's bottomless treasure box: seashells, berries, bees, vines, leaves, branches, nuts, and seeds. Inspirational poetry, favorite sayings, or scripture passages can be interwoven with pine cones, fruits, flowers, trees, stars, or animals! It is a great joy to choose your own personal language of motifs in a border, expressing your thoughts and feelings in a garland of carefully intertwined roses, herbs, butterflies, ribbons, or flying birds. Many elements can be strung together to create a border.

SHAPES OF BORDERS AND COMPOSITIONAL FORMATS

Now, let's talk about the many ways in which the border can be formed around the central image. In the image below, you can see a few of the compositional formats I frequently use in my woodburnings with border designs.

These include: an arch within a rectangle; an oval within a rectangle; a circle within a circle (including circular platters with scalloped edges and flat or beaded surfaces); a circle within a square; and vertical or landscape formats (rectangles within rectangles, or curved-corner rectangles within rectangles).

I enjoy creating little vignettes (small pictures or designs) to fill in the odd corners and curves created by nestling one shape within another. It is also fun to have the central image break through into the border area, or to have the border design break through into the central image. You can see an example of the border design breaking through into the central image area in the detail from the screech owl woodburning, shown on page 37.

Borders don't have to be boring. Simple outlines can become lace, rope, vines, tape

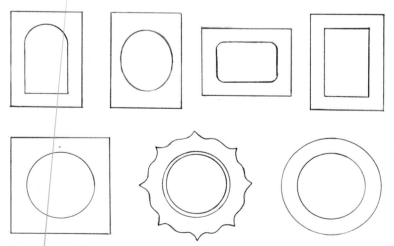

Compositional formats. A few of the compositional formats I frequently use in woodburnings with border designs: rectangular with arch; rectangular with oval; horizontal rectangle with rounded rectangle; rectangle within rectangle; square with circle; scalloped border with circle; and circle within circle.

Border incorporated with central image. This border design looks quite striking breaking through into the central image. Don't be afraid to experiment with the border's edges. (Detail from "All Things Wise and Wonderful.")

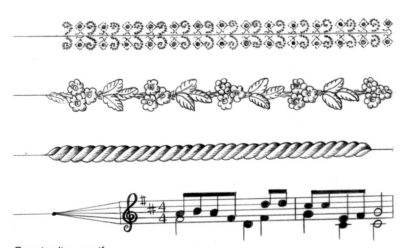

Creating line motifs. Transform a simple line into embroidery stitches, floral vines, rope, or a musical staff.

measures, or embroidery stitching. You use a border to define the edges of your central image and to tie the elements together. You can see many examples of this in the Complete Composition patterns section of the book (page 102).

As you have probably noticed, I especially love curved shapes, and I often enjoy working in a circular or oval format. You may prefer more geometric shapes, and you can choose a format that appeals to your sense of beauty and balance—the choices are infinite. Remember to do a few small, quick thumbnail sketches to help you visualize how your subject might look within each format.

Later on, as we begin to woodburn, you will learn strokes and special effects you can make with your woodburning tips that can be used to tie the various motifs in the border together. You will learn how to delicately burn along the edge of the platter to define the edges of the border. You can use the shading tip to create a subtle, burled wood look in the empty spaces between each element of the border. You will learn to use stippling, crosshatch, and basket weave patterns to fill spaces and unite the composition.

HOW A PATTERN COMES TOGETHER

A **pattern** is a composition drawn on tracing paper that can be transferred to the wood. As I have mentioned before, beginning with a full-size, carefully drawn pattern is the key to success in woodburning. Or at the very least, you can tape individual designs at the appropriate places on the wood and transfer them one at a time, if you prefer not to create a full pattern. The point is to not draw freehand on the wood because it is hard to erase major mistakes in pyrography—it's much better to make the mistakes on the tracing paper!

Persevere in your efforts to create your own personal patterns, even though it may seem difficult at first. The hours I have put into creating patterns have really paid off in enjoyment of the burning time, the flow of creativity, and the satisfaction of a comfort zone as I work, since the compositional problems have been worked out in advance. Of course, I will occasionally totally "wing it" in some pictures and make things up as I go along, but this is a *much* more difficult, stressful, and precarious way to work.

STEP 1: CHOOSE THE SIZE AND SHAPE OF YOUR WOOD

The first step is to decide if your composition will be designed for a round basswood platter, or a rectangular or square birch panel, or perhaps a wooden box lid, or other project. Once the size and shape of your wood are determined, you can proceed with planning your design.

STEP 2: CHOOSE THE CENTRAL IMAGE

Once you have decided on a central image or element pattern to be used in the central area of your composition, you can enlarge or reduce this image to fit the size of the wood. This can be done on a photocopier machine or by scanning the image into your computer, resizing it, and printing it out. Or you can trace the image using transparent tracing paper then enlarge or reduce it on a photocopier or computer. Photocopier machines are often available at office supply stores and libraries. The beauty of tracing paper is you can flip the pattern over and use the design in reverse as well.

STEP 3: DO YOU WANT TO ADD A BORDER?

Decide if you want a frame or border around your central image, and if so, proceed to choose the motifs you like from the elements patterns. Make tracings or photocopies of these patterns, and resize them to fit on your wood.

STEP 4: ARRANGING THE SEPARATE PARTS INTO A PATTERN

At this point, you have the choice of either making a master pattern sheet or simply taping each of the individual elements and the central image to your wood, and transferring each

separately. If the design is fairly simple, you can easily use the method of taping each individual pattern piece to the wood and then transferring. If the design is complex, I usually make a master pattern, so I can be sure all the parts work well together in a balanced composition.

Making a master pattern. To make a master pattern, cut a piece of tracing paper to the size of your wood piece, or trace your wood shape onto a larger sheet of tracing paper. Take all of the printed or traced elements and central image patterns, cut them out, and move them around on the tracing paper until you are happy with the composition and it seems balanced and satisfying. Using tracing paper enables you to draw lines where you need to and to connect or augment the images. You won't need to copy every little detail of the photographs you use as reference onto your master pattern. Focus on the main outlines and features, and indicate fur direction or feathers, etc., with short strokes as guides.

Tracing paper pattern sheet for "Young at Heart," taped to the wood and ready to transfer.

When you are satisfied, tape the cut-out images to the tracing paper with small pieces of transparent tape—just enough to hold them down, so that excess tape doesn't interfere with the transfer stage, later on.

STEP 5: TRANSFERRING YOUR DESIGN TO THE WOOD

The final step is to use graphite transfer paper, and transfer your design to the wood. This is a straightforward process and not nearly as time consuming as you might think.

After considering the wood grain (see sidebar, page 44), simply tape your master pattern securely to the wood at the top or side with masking tape. Slip your graphite transfer paper under the master pattern. Be sure that the graphite side is *facing down*. Many people like to use a red ballpoint pen so that they can see which lines they have gone over. Using your pen, carefully draw with slight pressure over all the lines in the pattern. Peek underneath the

graphite paper to check how dark your lines are coming out on the wood. Try to get them just dark enough to be clearly visible. Be careful that the pattern does not shift while you are working. Also, try not to rest the palm of your hand on the pattern because it will transfer large smudges of graphite onto the wood.

After removing the pattern and graphite paper, you can make use of your artists' kneaded eraser to clean up any smudges on the wood. **Suggestion:** It is very important to warm up the eraser in your hands or it will not work properly. To do this, stretch it out like Silly Putty and knead it like bread dough for at least thirty seconds. After doing this, you can press the kneaded eraser onto the smudges and lines to lighten them or very gently rub smudges cleanly away.

MAKING PATTERNS OF YOUR PETS FROM PHOTOGRAPHS

Making patterns of your pets from your own photographs is easy to do and does not require great drawing skills. On your computer, simply convert your photograph to black-and-white, and print it out on standard white paper at the size you need. You can use this copy as your pattern. If you are not comfortable with a computer, simply bring your photograph to a facility with a copier and enlarge it, in black and white, to the size you need. Then simply slip a piece of graphite paper underneath and transfer the image to the wood.

If you do enjoy drawing and feel confident with your skills, you can use a drawing as a pattern that can then be woodburned. As an example, on page 43 is a drawing I did of my daughter, Laura, when she was a baby. The drawing was done with graphite drawing pencils. I did have to readjust the details of her dress in order to clarify the lines for the

Pattern transfer for "Young at Heart."

Photograph of Snow Bear.

Pattern transfer of the photograph of SnowBear.

woodburning. I found a dress I liked, stuffed it with plastic bags to create a model, and redrew the dress for the woodburning.

A full-color painting can also be converted into a black and white pattern and used to create a woodburning. For example, I made the painting of my daughter, Rachel (page 43), with oil paints on illustration board. I had to add much more detail to the border to create the woodburning, since woodburnings are so detailed.

Completed woodburning of "Snow Bear."

Graphite drawing for "Pleasant Dreams."

Completed woodburning of "Pleasant Dreams."

Oil painting for "Ode to Joy."

Completed woodburning of "Ode to Joy."

Partially completed woodburning of "Ode to Joy," with the pencil transfer lines still showing on the unburned parts.

THOUGHTS ON WORKING WITH WOOD GRAIN

One of the things we woodburning artists cannot change is the fact the WOOD HAS GRAIN! Wood is not a flat, white, perfect, manmade, commercially manufactured surface like paper, canvas, or gesso board. Sometimes, no matter how carefully you lay out your pattern so that your design will work harmoniously with the wood grain or knot patterns, the wood grain will make its presence known loud and clear in spite of your best efforts. As you can see in the examples here, the grain lines are quite visible.

Woodburning can sometimes seem like a contest to overcome the effects of the wood grain, and sometimes, the grain "wins." I have learned, after many such power struggles, that it's best to stop fighting with the grain and accept that this is one of "the things I cannot change." Nor would I want to.

That being said, it is important to consider the way you line up your pattern with the grain lines before transferring the pattern. This means simply thinking about which direction most of the texture lines will be going (for example, fur lines). If it is possible to get the majority of the texture lines to flow in the same direction as the wood grain, rather than crossing in a perpendicular path over the grain lines, this is preferable, though not always possible. Just do the best you can to line up the grain in a way that makes the most sense, as you consider how your burning lines will cross the grain.

Effects of wood grain. Detail from "A Little Nut."

Effects of wood grain. Detail from "Kind Hearts Are Gardens."

Effects of wood grain. Detail from "The Loveliest of All was the Unicorn."

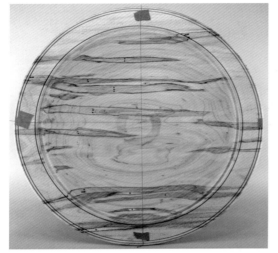

Grain lines in the ambrosia maple platter before woodburning.

The tracing paper pattern for the ambrosia maple platter with the grain lines indicated and the design sketched.

The completed ambrosia maple platter with the thirds mixture wood finish applied.

CREATIVE USE OF GRAIN LINES

Some woods can have strong lines and distinctive markings that only add to their uniqueness. A woodturning friend gave me an unfinished hand-turned ambrosia maple platter as a gift. The holes and subtly colored streaks are made by the ambrosia beetle as it bores into the maple tree.

It was a real challenge to design a woodburning composition on such a special piece. I did not want to cover up any of the amazing natural markings with my design. My goal was to choose a simple composition that would allow the beauty of the wood itself to shine through. I chose a quiet landscape subject because to me the markings suggested wispy elongated clouds and flowing fields. I first traced the grain patterns on a piece of tracing paper, and designed my landscape on that paper. I placed my pattern horizontally, coordinating with the grain lines. I then transferred and woodburned my design, as you can see at left. The taped thread helps me clearly establish my vertical and horizontal orientation.

Chapter 3:
PRACTICE PROJECTS

To help you become comfortable with your woodburner and tips, I have designed two practice projects students have enjoyed. Just as athletes, dancers, musicians, and singers must do warm-up exercises and practice constantly, it is helpful for the artist to do exploratory projects to learn the full range of expression possible with his or her tools and materials.

OVERVIEW OF THE PROJECTS

The two exercises in this chapter will help you learn the capabilities of each of the five recommended tips. As an added bonus, you will have two beautiful and impressive reference charts to hang on your studio wall! The first project is the Crazy Quilt Sampler, and the second is the Four Basic Shapes. Let's discuss a few basic techniques before we begin.

TECHNIQUE

For those of you who are beginners, let's start with some simple line strokes on scrap pieces of basswood or birch plywood. It's always a good idea to practice your strokes on scrap wood first when working on a project. Save small scrap pieces of ¼" (6mm) birch plywood or whatever wood on which you are working. Test the point of your woodburning tool on the scraps, and experiment with different heat settings until you are sure you can produce the effect you want. This will reduce the risk of spoiling your work.

To keep your tips clean as you work, keep a small piece of fine sandpaper handy (200 grit or higher) or a fine-grit sandpaper type nail file (220-320 grit). Use it to clean carbon build-up from your burning tips as you work. Shut off the burner and let the tip cool for a few minutes before cleaning it. You will know if your tip needs cleaning if the tip drags or skips on the wood, or if it makes inconsistently burned lines. It is not difficult to keep your tips clean, and for finely detailed work, it is essential. Simply stroke the cooled tip on all sides across the sandpaper or nail file. It's that easy!

Let's go over a few basics as you prepare to begin woodburning. How you hold the woodburning pen hand piece is important and a matter of personal choice. I hold my woodburning pen just as I would a pencil.

Practice board. Use practice boards to experiment with the full range of textures and lines you can create.

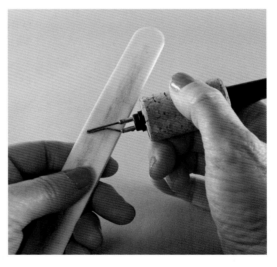

Cleaning a woodburning tip with a sandpaper-type nail file.

Holding the woodburning pen.

Experiment with extending your pinky finger on the work surface to balance your hand, or try keeping it curled under your hand. Do what is most comfortable for you. Some people prefer to hold the pen in the "sketching position," with the index and middle fingers extended full-length on the pen, and the thumb underneath. I find this position awkward, but some students prefer it.

Experiment with moving the pen tip forward and backward on the wood surface with your fingers, without moving the rest of your hand. Get the feel of the pen in your hand and be aware of how the cord moves as you move the pen. Always be sure to keep the cord away from the hot tip. Learn to hold your pen lightly; squeezing too hard will make your fingers ache and your hand hot.

If Einstein were a woodcrafter and he were to write an equation for woodburners, it would not be $E=mc^2$. Instead, (tongue firmly "in cheek"), it might be something like this:

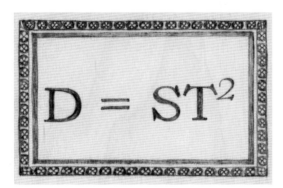

What I mean by this is that D (the darkness and depth of the line you create) will depend on these variables:

S is the *softness* or hardness of the wood you have selected for your project. For example, pine is a soft wood and will burn much more easily than a close-grained, harder wood like birch or maple.

T^2 is the *temperature* at which you have set the woodburner's heat control knob. And the

TIP Remember to position your work piece so that you can pull the stroke toward you as you make the lines. This will give you much more control, accuracy, and comfort. I am constantly moving my piece of wood to a position that makes it easier to burn the lines. One of the biggest mistakes beginners make is to always keep their wood in the same position. Don't be afraid to move your wood around to get the right angle or position for burning comfortably.

amount of time the pen tip spends touching the wood, which is controlled by the speed at which you move the pen tip. (The slower you move the heated tip on the wood, the darker the line.)

To illustrate this, try an experiment on a piece of scrap wood.

Using your C-1 (small calligraphy) tip, set your woodburner (if you have a variable temperature machine) to a medium setting. On the Colwood Detailer, I would use setting 6 or 7. Now, make a series of straight lines, using the corner edge of the U shape of the tip. Starting at the top of the line and pulling the pen tip toward you, move the tip on the wood from top to bottom. You can see these lines on my practice board on page 48.

Time. If you move at a slow speed as you come down onto the wood, your line will be darker at the top than at the bottom, and you may find you create a little burned hole or crater at the beginning of the line. You can see these holes in the three lines drawn on the left hand side on my practice board. In woodburners' lingo, this is called a "blob" (or "the dreaded blob!"). It can also happen if you slow down or pause mid-line. To avoid this, try gliding smoothly at a consistent speed, and then lifting off smoothly at the end of the line, like a hawk catching a fish.

With practice, you will be able to make a smooth line. Don't get too frustrated by gouges and blobs—there are simple ways to fix them, which we will cover in the next section.

Temperature. Now let's experiment with raising and lowering the temperature. You will find that at the highest heat settings (8-10), your tip will glow red-hot. No matter how quickly you move it, the tip will flare and scorch the wood. At the lowest heat settings (1-4), you will hardly be able to make any mark at all.

With practice, you will learn to coordinate time (the speed of your hand) and the temperature setting with the softness or hardness of the wood. It won't take long before you are able to create a consistent burn depth and darkness. Remember that experimenting and making mistakes is the best way to learn anything new—relax, have fun, and enjoy yourself!

It is not necessary to use a lot of pressure on the woodburning tip to create darker lines. Pressure should be light—keep experimenting with the temperature settings of the woodburner and your speed to control the darkness and depth of the burn, rather than resorting to pushing down hard on the tip, which can quickly cause hand and finger strain.

FIXING MISTAKES AND COMMON PROBLEMS

Many of the burning techniques I use have been discovered by accident and experimentation. I've done a lot of scraping and sanding of mistakes over the years! You will be surprised to learn that wood can be quite forgiving.

Fixing mistakes. My best woodburning friend is my little X-acto knife (hobby blade). I like the kind with the snap-off blade sections—

when it starts to get dull, simply take pliers and break off a ¼" (6mm) section along the grooved lines, and voila!—you have a fresh, sharp edge.

I use it to scrape off mistakes, lighten an area that was too darkly burned and pick out highlights. I even use it to scrape animal whiskers, chipmunk stripes, grass, or stars into a darker background. I can soften fur outlines and make them look more natural. I find the blade works *much* better than sandpaper to erase mistakes because it does a cleaner job. Also, using a knife blade is much more precise than sanding. Sandpaper can leave an uneven surface over a large area, but the scraper can remove a burned line without removing the wood surrounding it. Overuse of sandpaper can change the texture of the wood so that the sanded area does not accept stain or paint in quite the same way. The knife will not affect the wood's texture as much.

Always remember to gently scrape away many shallow layers, rather than gouging the wood or trying to remove the mistake in just a few strokes. Also, be aware that the top birch layer on birch plywood is approximately ¹⁄₃₂" thick, so scrape gently to avoid piercing through to the under layer.

Blobs. If you hesitate just after the tip touches the wood, you will find that your lines are darker at the top, with a blob or crater at the start and maybe even at the finish of the line. With a little practice, this problem can be overcome by considering your motion and speed. Your tip is the hottest when it first touches the wood, and the trick to overcoming this is to make sure the tip is in motion as it "lands," and then adjust your speed to maintain a consistent burn depth and darkness. Always keep the tip in motion from the point of contact to the "lift off." The tip should glide lightly and smoothly.

A PERSONAL EXAMPLE OF FIXING A MAJOR MISTAKE

Occasionally I will make a serious mistake on a large area of the wood, as I did while working on the woodburning "Peace." I was having so much fun burning the lion's mane that I didn't realize until I finally stepped back from my work and looked at it from a distance (do this often!) that he looked like he had a huge Elvis pompadour or had just come from the beauty parlor. I call him the Liberace Lion, whom some of you may remember as the famous pianist with the mountain of hair.

Here's a case where you must *carefully* use a sander to erase your mistake, which is quite scary to do on birch plywood. If you sand down to the under layer, you're sunk! Fortunately, I was able to get *most* of the lines off, although I had burned them in so deeply, they were still visible after sanding. Rather than taking a chance on sanding any deeper, I decided to add a thick grove of trees and foliage behind the lion to hide the lines, which worked well, although they are still visible. Sometimes mistakes will lead you to solutions that work even better for your picture. I was originally planning to have a plain, quiet sky area in the outer border. But the trees added a lot to the woodburning, and I wouldn't have added them if I hadn't bungled the lion's mane. No one has ever mentioned the strange curvy lines in the trees behind the lion's head!

The "Liberace" lion.

"Peace," the completed woodburning.

Bent points. Sometimes the heated point of your woodburning pen will bend. No problem—after shutting off the woodburner and letting the tip cool slightly, just turn the point around, and press it gently back into position on a scrap piece of wood from the opposite direction. This can also be done gently with pliers.

Scorch marks. If the heat is set too high, the tip will burn an uneven line with golden scorch marks along the edges. Scraping with a blade will help to clean up the edges a little, but it is hard to completely get rid of scorch marks. Practice on scrap wood to establish the correct heat setting and hand speed that you need to burn a nice, neat line, without scorching.

PRACTICE PROJECT #1
CRAZY QUILT SAMPLER

Dealing with wood grain. As I discussed in Chapter 1, the grain lines in wood can burn differently from the surrounding wood, either lighter or darker. Try adjusting your tip speed as you cross the grain. If the grain is softer than the surrounding areas, you will have to speed up to prevent the line from becoming darker. If the grain is harder than the surrounding areas, you will have to slow down to prevent the line from becoming too light. Sometimes you may have to go back over the grain areas and do additional burning to even out the areas you have burned. Don't forget, you can always use your knife blade to scrape areas of your lines that are too dark.

Adjust your heat dial for each different burning tip that you use. Each tip will require a different heat setting to create the same effects. Practice on your practice scraps! One tip may burn very dark at 7, while another tip will need to be set at 8.5 to achieve the same degree of darkness. I sometimes burn with my right hand holding my burning tip, and my left hand constantly adjusting the heat setting knob. Different areas of the wood will require different heat settings as well, as the density of the grain varies. Be prepared to constantly adjust your heat setting as you become more proficient.

Goal. To learn the capabilities of each tip, and to build a vocabulary of textures that you can use in your woodburnings.

To encourage you to relax and see this exercise as a fun learning opportunity, I have intentionally made my examples in each square of the sampler rather loose. The computer and magazine images that we are all bombarded with are so perfect and airbrushed, I find that it's always good to remind ourselves, as artists, that we are *not* computers. It's okay to have rough areas and inconsistencies in our work—it adds to the charm and handmade quality of the woodburnings. Woodburning has long been considered to be a rustic, natural type of folk art, so we can always claim that our errors are intended to add to the rustic quality! Be patient and tolerant with yourself in this learning stage; we often learn more from our mistakes than from our successes.

The examples I've given for each square of the sampler are simply suggestions to guide you. Please feel free to discover and use variations on them or to experiment with your own lines, patterns, and textures in the sampler blocks.

In the photos on page 54, you can see several samplers completed by students in one of my woodburning classes. Notice how each has its own unique personality. Feel free to be creative as you complete your own sampler.

TRANSFERRING THE PATTERN

After enlarging or reducing the size of the Crazy Quilt Sampler pattern to fit your wood, transfer the design to the wood piece you have chosen using graphite transfer paper. You can use a ruler to guide your pen as you transfer the straight lines from the pattern. Try not to rest the palm of your hand on the pattern to avoid excess graphite being inadvertently

"Crazy Quilt Sampler"
practice project #1.

transferred to the wood surface. Don't forget to sand your wood before transferring the pattern.

My sampler was done on a 12" x 12" (305 x 305mm) piece of Baltic birch. I lined up my pattern with the grain, so that the grain *runs vertically* from top to bottom. Remember, the direction of the grain lines will strongly affect the lines you burn.

Outline the squares with the corner of your C-1 tip, or with your C (writing) tip if you are more comfortable with that. You can outline just a few blocks at a time rather than burning all the lines at once. Although using a ruler when transferring the pattern is helpful, for this woodburning stage, you do not need to use a ruler. Don't worry about making the woodburned outlines perfectly straight—once all of the blocks are filled in, it will not matter if the lines are slightly wavy. You can make the lines medium dark for now. After you have completed all the blocks in the sampler and textured the edges, you can go back and darken all of the lines with your C-1 tip. Relax and let yourself enjoy the adventure of learning to woodburn!

Now with your C tip, label the rows numerically and alphabetically as shown. If you prefer a finer line, use the Micro C tip.

C-1 SMALL CALLIGRAPHY TIP

Let's begin our sampler with the first three rows on the left hand side, which will all be done with the C-1 tip. Remember the goal is to learn, not to create perfect squares or to exactly copy my examples.

The C 1 small calligraphy tip.

This extremely useful tip is actually three tips in one. When using the corner of the tip, it performs like the C (writing tip). When used with the wide edge held horizontally on the burning surface, it can be used to make broad areas of shading. When held at a 45° angle to the wood and rotated between the thumb and fingers, it can be used as a calligraphy tip, creating gracefully curved thin and thick lines.

A-1 checkerboard. Lightly pencil in guidelines to create the checkerboard pattern so that the squares will be evenly spaced. Constantly experiment with your heat setting to learn to control how dark or light you make your lines. Practice on your scrap wood first. Remember to clean your tip often if it drags or burns unevenly.

Student samplers from the 2009 John C. Campbell Folk School woodburning class.

Pattern for the "Crazy Quilt Sampler." Enlarge 200% for actual size.

Using the entire *wide edge* of the tip, make the dark squares. Now, using the corner edge, draw the light vertical lines in each light square of the checkerboard. Don't forget that you can gently use your scraper knife to lighten areas that may burn too darkly.

A-2 parallel lines. These are straight, freehand lines, all stroking in the same direction. Again, using the corner edge of the C-1 tip, draw vertical lines from top to bottom of the square, close together. Go more slowly at the top half and use slightly more pressure, to make the line darker. Let your line become lighter toward the bottom half by stroking faster, with less pressure. Always be sure to pull the stroke toward you, and then lightly "lift off" at the bottom of the stroke. This should create a lighter, thinner line toward the bottom of the square.

A-3 interwoven strokes. This square is similar to large, thick crosshatching and will help you practice going across the wood grain. With the tip on its wide side edge, stroke

horizontally in 5 or 6 stripes across the square. Then repeat this motion vertically to create a criss-cross effect.

A-4 stippling (dots). Stippling is the use of dots to create shadows, textures, and 3-D effects in images. The effect is created by tapping the corner edge of the C-1 tip on the wood at a 45° angle. Experiment with dots and short dashes on different heat settings, closer together or further apart.

A-5 short strokes. Remember to position your wood so you can pull the pen strokes *toward* you. Make short or longer lines, slightly curved, going in the same direction, and slightly overlapping or askew, rather than strictly parallel. This technique is useful for fur lines, short grass, and hair. To make fur look natural, be sure to curve each stroke to follow the contours of the animal's body.

A-6 stone path. Use the wide edge of the tip on high heat to create random shapes separated by thin, unburned areas of wood.

A-7 fine crosshatch. Crosshatching is two groups of parallel lines that are perpendicular to each other. Learning to crosshatch will teach you a handy way to create shading, texture, shadows, and depth in your work. Turn your wood so you can pull the tip toward you.

A-8 curves. Practicing curved lines will help you develop control and flexibility of your pen tip. As you progress through the curve, roll the pen between your thumb and fingers. Use the *wide edge* of the tip, and move it from side to side in a smooth motion, angling it as you make the turns.

A-9 concentric circles. Begin by filling in the four corners of the square with short, curved strokes, rotating the wood so the pen tip pulls toward you as you make the curved lines. After filling in the four corners, which creates a blank circle in the center, make short, curved connecting strokes, working toward the center from the outside of the circle. There is no need to try to draw the whole spiral all in one stroke.

A-10 small fish scales stroke. This is a curved, hooked stroke, using the corner edge of the tip. The curve and backstroke use a bit more of the *wide edge*, and hence, this part of the line is darker and wider. Holding the pen so the corner edge touches the wood, move the tip to the left, making the thinner line. Then curve down and around the C-shaped hook, and then back to the right. On the C curve and back stroke, make the line wider by using the wide edge of the tip, and holding the tip down longer.

B-1 triple crosshatch. This stroke can be used in the darkest, shaded areas of your woodburnings to create depth and texture. On top of the regular perpendicular crosshatching, (as in A-7), add an additional layer of diagonal woodburned lines using the corner of the tip.

B-2 wavy, curved lines. Roll the pen between your thumb and fingers, using the corner of the tip. Wavy lines are useful for depicting the grainy patterns of wood or the rippled patterns on water.

B-3 short, overlapped dashes. Using the corner of the tip, make heavy layers of short dashes, leaving the inner circle lighter than the edges to create a 3-D effect.

B-4 random dashes with "tails". Here's your chance to make blobs on purpose! Hit the wood hard with the tip corner and trail off lightly to make the tails. Turn your work as you go, and aim for a random pattern.

B-5 basket weave pattern. This is a handy texturing pattern for filling in blank areas on borders. Draw the horizontal and vertical guidelines lightly in pencil first. For more definition, darken the striped lines of each tiny basket weave square on one side only.

B-6 large dots. Using the corner of the tip,

experiment with raising and lowering the heat setting to intentionally create a light golden brown halo of "scorch" surrounding each dot.

B-7 nine block cross. The dark squares are made from vertical lines burned close together on a high heat setting. The lighter squares are created with lightly burned lines drawn further apart, on a lower heat setting.

B-8 curved line basket weave. This is a random design of interesting, curved lines.

B-9 diagonal criss cross. Use the *wide edge* of the tip, making lengthwise lines from corner to corner.

B-10 feathers. Position your wood upside-down so you can pull the strokes toward you. First, make three long, slightly curved lines. These will be the central quill lines of the three feathers. Beginning from the central lines, use the corner of your tip to make short, curved feather vane lines. Do not outline the feather edge.

C-1 wavy lines. This square is similar to B-2, with even thicker and thinner lines and is useful for depicting wood grain or water ripples. Use the corner edge of the tip but roll slightly to left and right, onto the wider edge, as you make the curves.

C-2 large fish scale. Follow the directions given in A-10. After laying in all the scales, go back in with the corner of the tip and make shaded parallel lines at the base of each "scale" to add depth and dimension.

C-3 wide-thin pattern. Draw the shapes with the corner of the tip and fill in with parallel lines.

C-4 curved contour lines crosshatch. Contour lines, made with the corner of the tip, follow the shape of the object—great for depicting rounded objects.

C-7 fur lines. Short, diagonal strokes made with the corner of the tip.

C-8 wavy lines. Gently roll the wide edge of the tip between thumb and fingers *as you pull the pen toward you.*

C-9 leaf pattern. This square uses a technique similar to the one used in creating feathers in B-10. *Turn your board upside-down so you can pull the pen toward you* as you burn the lines. Outline the leaf shapes. Draw in the central leaf veins. Make curved lines, gracefully radiating outward from the central vein to the leaf edge with the corner of the tip.

C-10 diagonal dashes. Use the corner of the tip to make quick movements, setting the tip down and lifting off.

MINI J TIP (MINI 'TIGHT ROUND')

The edge of the rounded tip of the Mini J allows you to easily make straight or curved lines in a tight radius, and it can also be laid flat on its side and used as a shader in tight spaces.

D-1 random squiggles. Make these using the thin edge of the tip, held at an 80° angle to the wood.

D-2 diagonal wide lines. Hold the pen at a 45° angle to the wood, using the flat surface of the tip, laid on its side.

D-3 vertical lines. These lines are drawn from top to bottom using the thin edge of the tip.

D-8 crisscross lines. The lines are made with the tip flat on its side.

D-9 checkerboard. The vertical lines in the darker squares are made with the edge of the tip with higher heat and with the lines closer together. The horizontal lines in the lighter squares are made with lower heat and with the lines further apart.

D-10 curved wavy lines. The thin edge and the flat surface of the tip are used in each line by rotating the tip between your thumb and fingers as you move across the wood grain.

The Mini J "tight round" tip.

E-1 vertical wavy lines. To create a halo effect of light golden "scorch," turn up the heat and make vertical lines while rolling the pen between your fingers so you alternate using the wide edge and thin edge of the Mini J tip.

E-2 spiral. Using the thin edge of the tip and beginning at the four outer corners, first make thin, curved lines in each corner, which will create a blank circle in the middle. Then, rotating the wood, make short, curved connecting strokes until you reach the center.

E-9 vertical lines. Move the tip more slowly at the bottom of the line to darken as you pull the tip toward you.

E-10 stippling dots. Hold the thin edge of the tip at an 80° to 90° angle to the wood and tap to create dots.

F-1 diagonal dashes with light gold "scorch" halo effect. Turn up the heat a bit to get the halo effect.

F-2 leaf shapes. Outline the shapes with the thin edge of the tip and fill in with the flat edge.

F-9 stone path. Outline the shapes with the thin edge and fill in with the flat edge on a higher heat setting.

F-10 curved contour lines. This square was created using the thin edge of the tip.

THE MC TIP (MICRO C)

This tip writes just like a fine ballpoint pen. It glides along the surface of the wood, and is useful for very fine details, including lettering, signatures and shading.

G-1 alphabet. Practice creating letters with the MC tip.

The MC (Micro C) tip.

G-2 light vertical lines. These lines are drawn from top to bottom.

G-3 fish scales. Make a curved, hooked stroke.

G-8 fine crosshatch. Draw horizontal and vertical lines to create a crosshatch pattern.

G-9 fine basket weave. Squares with vertical lines are alternated with squares with horizontal lines. Emphasize the thickness of the lines on one edge of each tiny square to create dimensionality.

G-10 wavy lines in random patterns. This pattern is handy for depicting wood grain and water ripples.

THE C ('WRITING') TIP

The C writing tip is just like the Micro C tip except that it has more of a curved surface to work with and is larger.

H-1 curved contour lines. These lines are made darker at the edge by going slower and using slightly more pressure. Keep the lines in the center area lighter.

H-2 brick pattern. Outline the bricks first and then fill in with dark lines close together. If you accidentally burn too far into the light area between the bricks, gently scrape these areas to lighten them.

H-3 semi-circles converging in the center. This is a random pattern designed to help you practice curved lines.

H-4 diagonal lines. These are simple diagonal lines running from corner to corner.

H-7 wide-thin pattern. Outline the shapes and fill in with dark lines close together.

H-8 overlapping waves. This is an attractive pattern created with curved, overlapped lines.

H-9 textured flagstone. Outline the "flagstones" and stipple inside the shapes. Fill in the dark areas between the stones with short, dark lines, close together.

H-10 large fish scales. Each "scale" is shaded with parallel lines at its base to indicate overlapping and create a sense of depth.

I-1 herringbone pattern. This is a simple line pattern filled in with short lines going in opposite directions.

I-2 your initial. Lightly sketch your initial in pencil. Leave the inside area of the letter blank, and surround it with stippling.

I-3 crosshatch. This is a simple crosshatch pattern, useful for many applications.

I-4 spiral. Begin by filling in the four corners of the square with short, curved strokes, rotating the wood so the pen tip pulls toward you as you make the curved lines. After filling in the four corners, which creates a blank circle in the center, make short curved connecting strokes working toward the center from the outside of the circle. Don't try to draw the spiral line all in one stroke.

I-5 curved line basket weave. This pattern is made by alternating two-strand and three-strand basket weave and using curved lines between the woven areas.

I-6 stippling dots. The dots are created with the tip held at an 80° to 90° angle to the wood and tapping.

I-7 grass clumps. Turn the sampler upside-down and pull the tip toward you in short, curved strokes, to create "clumps of grass."

The C "writing" tip.

I-8 wavy lines. Move your whole hand and the pen tip in graceful, curving motions to create the wavy lines.

I-9 random cross pattern. These lines are created by simply "writing" with the woodburning tip as you would with a pen. Do be careful to touch down lightly and lift off gently to prevent blobs.

I-10 horizontal broken dash lines. Keep the heat setting on medium low to prevent blobbing and scorching as you burn the short dashes.

THE S 'SHADING' TIP

The curved, flat edge of the shader can create a huge variety of effects and can cover large areas of shading quickly and smoothly. Experiment with different heat settings.

J-1 star. Using the flat, curved surface of the tip and rotating the wood as you proceed, pull shaded bands of woodburning from the outer edge of the square toward the center, leaving the center area lighter. Then, using your scraper, scrape rays of light coming from the central light area and extending into the dark shaded areas. This is very dramatic in night scenes.

J-2 random swirls. The swirls are created with the flat, curved surface of the shader.

J-3 wavy vertical lines. The wavy lines are made with the flat, curved surface of the tip.

J-4 stippling dots and dashes. Hold the shader upside-down, with the tip at an 80° to 90° angle to the wood, and tap on the surface, at a low heat setting, to keep the effect light and delicate.

J-5 crisscross. Horizontal and vertical bands created with the flat, curved surface of the shader.

J-6 soft feathers. Turn the wood sideways so you can pull the shader tip toward you. Make the central quill line of each feather with the

The S "shading" tip.

tip of the shader. Then, using the flat, curved surface of the tip, gently make curved lines to represent the feather vanes coming from the central quill line. Straight lines on feathers will look unnatural.

J-7 large fish scales. Use the flat, curved surface to create curved, hooked shapes.

J-8 wavy lines. This is a random pattern created with the flat, curved surface of the shader. Vary the pressure and the speed at which you move the tip to get the dark and light effects in each line.

J-9 checkerboard pattern. The darker squares are made with the flat, curved surface of the shader. The lighter squares are done with the upside-down tip of the shader used to make vertical lines. You can also draw the lines around each of the small squares with the upside-down tip.

J-10 overlapping waves. Use the flat, curved surface of the shader to draw the curved lines of the waves.

FINISHING TOUCHES ON THE CRAZY QUILT SAMPLER PROJECT

Using the flat, curved surface of the S tip, burn a dark border around the outer edge of the wood, to give a more finished look to the piece. Notice how much easier it is to burn in the direction of the grain rather than across the grain. Clean your tip frequently if it stops burning evenly.

I created an antiqued "burled" wood effect on the border of the sampler by lightly gliding the flat, curved surface of the S tip

PRACTICE PROJECT #2
FOUR BASIC SHAPES

over the entire outer border area. This creates an interesting texture and makes the sampler look old and weathered. It's a useful way to tie together elements in your borders. Start out at a low-heat setting, and slowly increase the temperature to achieve the level of darkness you desire in the border texture. If you burn some areas too darkly, a gentle rubbing with a piece of sandpaper will lighten the area.

Now that you have completed all of the squares and textured the border, you can go back to darken and redefine the lines around each square of the sampler with the corner of your C-1 tip, if you desire.

To prepare the central circle for the color exercise, woodburn the outlines of the eight pie-shaped wedges within the circle with your C-1 or C tip. You can use my flower design pattern or create your own design for the central circular area. Apply color washes over the woodburned lines. Feel free to add striped lines, stippling, or other textures of your choice to each pie wedge. Then, with your Micro C tip, write in the names of the eight colors we will be using in each wedge. (For more information on using watercolor washes to add color to your Crazy Quilt Sampler, please see page 64.)

Four basic shapes for the woodburning practice project #2.

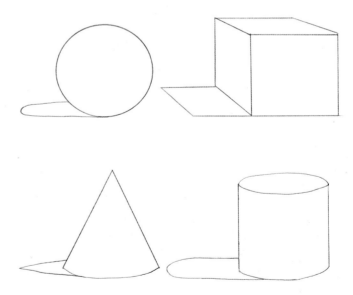

Pattern for four basic shapes project. Enlarge 200% for actual size.

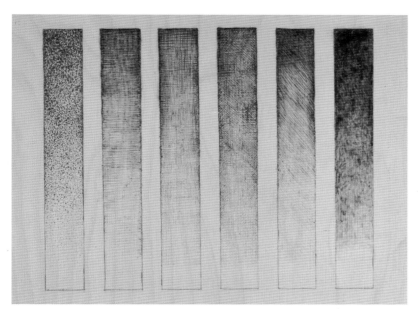

Woodburned value scale chart of shading and texturing effects

Goal. To apply techniques such as stippling and crosshatching learned in the Crazy Quilt Sampler project and to create three-dimensional shapes with shading and cast shadows.

First, sand an 8" (203mm) square piece of Baltic birch or basswood. Study the grain pattern, then tape the pattern (see pattern illustration on page 60) securely in place and transfer the pattern to the wood with graphite transfer paper.

Use very light pressure with your pen as you transfer—just enough to leave a light guideline. You can use a ruler to guide your pen as you transfer the pattern, to make the straight lines. Keep the transferred cast shadow outlines very light; a visible pencil outline around the cast shadow area will not look realistic and may not be easy to erase before beginning the woodburning.

When transferring, try not to rest the side or palm of your hand on the graphite paper to avoid unwanted smudges of graphite on the wood. After transferring is complete, use your (warmed up!) kneaded eraser to lighten the guidelines as much as possible and remove smudges. Wipe the wood surface clean with a soft lint-free cloth.

Before beginning the actual woodburning work, take a moment to study the woodburned value scale chart (left).

All of the tonal values in this chart were created with the woodburning tips only; no watercolor stain has been applied. The shading and texturing effects were created with the following tips:

Row 1: Stippling dots. The darkest areas were done with the C tip on higher heat settings. The lighter areas were done with the Micro C tip on lower heat settings.

Row 2: Parallel lines. These were created with the same tips and heat settings used for stippling dots in Row 1, using the C tip in the darkest areas and the Micro C in the light areas.

Row 3: Two-layer crosshatch. The darkest areas can be made with either the C-1 tip or the Mini J tip, whichever is most comfortable for you. The middle area was done with the C tip and the lightest area with the Micro C tip. Be sure to vary the heat settings as needed with each tip.

Row 4: Four-layer crosshatch. This row was created with the same techniques and tips used in two-layer crosshatch.

Row 5: Short, overlapped fur lines. The darkest areas were created with the C-1 tip or the Mini J tip (using the sharp edge). The C tip was used for the middle area. The lightest area was created with the Micro C tip.

Row 6: "Burled wood" antiqued effect. This effect was created by moving the S tip in small, circular motions, with the highest heat settings and slightly more pressure on the tip used in the darkest areas, and very low heat settings and a gentle, soft touch in the lightest areas.

This chart illustrates how to make very gradual transitions from the lightest areas of highlights to the darkest areas. As you woodburn across a curved, rounded surface, (as with a sphere, cone, or cylinder), strive for a seamless transition from dark to light, rather than a striped effect of dark, medium, and light tones. Making a value scale chart is a simple and fun exercise you could try on your own for extra practice.

STEP 1: OUTLINE SHAPES AND CREATE FORM WITH BASIC TONE

Your project may look kind of bland and unexciting at first, but be patient. Step 2 will add drama and contrast. Artists often find their projects can have a disheartening period about midway through, when it's hard to visualize the finished project. Just stick with it, and you'll be rewarded for your perseverance.

Sphere. With the Micro C tip, outline the form. I have made the artistic decision that the light is coming from the upper right, so I am keeping the outlines on the right upper side very light. I have left the areas of the wood where the light hits the object completely bare, so that those areas will remain lightest in value.

Beginning with the Micro C tip, make the lightest dots next to the highlight (unburned area) and work down toward the side and bottom left. Keep the tone even. Experiment on scrap wood with different heat settings. Notice how just this simple overall light tone already begins to create realism and the illusion of three dimensions.

Cube. With the Micro C tip, make light crosshatched vertical and horizontal lines across the front and left side areas. Leave the

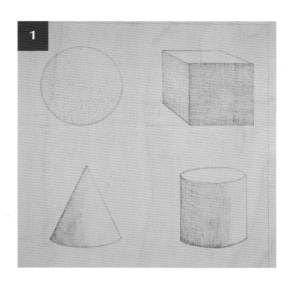

STEP 1. Outline and basic tone.

top of the cube as unburned wood, to indicate where the light is hitting the surface.

Cone. With the Micro C tip, make horizontal, *curved* contour lines following the rounded shape of the cone. Pull strokes from the outline on the left toward the center. Turn the wood as you work, so that you can always pull the woodburning tip toward you.

Cylinder. With the Micro C tip, make horizontal, *curved* contour lines. Then overlap these with straight vertical crosshatched lines.

STEP 2: SHADING

Please refer to the illustration as you proceed with adding shading to the four basic shapes.

Sphere. Using the C tip, which makes a bigger, darker dot than the Micro C tip, build up the stippling pattern, gradually becoming lighter and less dense as you transition toward the highlight. You can use the folded corner of a piece of 220-grit sandpaper to lighten any areas that get too dark, or gently scrape the area with your knife. Darken the outline on the shaded side and bottom edge of the sphere, and blend the dots on the dark side into the dark outline.

Cube. With the C tip, darken the horizontal and vertical crosshatched lines on the left side, and darken the outlines along the left sides and bottom of the cube. Then, add a third layer of diagonal crosshatched lines on the left side of the cube. Remember to turn the wood so you can pull the strokes toward you.

Cone. With the curved, sharp edge of the Mini-J tip, darken the straight line on the left side and bottom edge of the cone. Then, again using the curved edge of the Mini-J tip, strengthen and build up the curved lines starting at the left side and pulling toward you, lightening and "lifting off" at the end of the stroke. You can also use the wide, flat edge of the Mini-J tip to emphasize the deepest shading on the left side.

Cylinder. Just as you did with the cone, use the sharp edge and the wide flat edge of the Mini-J tip to first strengthen the outlines on the left and bottom of the cylinder, and then shade from dark to light across its surface. Remember to curve the horizontal lines to indicate the rounded contour of the cylinder. The vertical shading lines are straight lines.

On all of the shapes, don't worry about random darker areas that appear due to grain lines. These can be evened out and blended later on with a wash of burnt umber or Van Dyke Brown watercolor applied to the deepest

shadow side, and a light, blotted watercolor wash transitioning toward the lighter side. Leave the lightest, highlighted areas as bare wood, with no wash or woodburning at all. You may need to reburn a few lines after applying the watercolor wash. Use a hairdryer to completely dry the color wash, before reburning. (See Adding Color with Watercolor Washes on page 64.)

STEP 3: CAST SHADOWS

It is important to remember that outlining a cast shadow will not look natural. The cast shadow is shaped like the object itself but appears narrowed because it is lying flat and is seen in perspective. To distinguish the object from the shadow it casts, make the cast shadow either somewhat lighter or somewhat darker in tone than the shading on the object, and strengthen the outline between the object and the shadow to separate them along the edge of the shape.

As you work on Step 3, refer to the completed Four Basic Shapes woodburning on page 60.

Sphere. Make dots with the C tip; the dots will become less dense as the shadow gets further away from the sphere. Do not outline the shadow area.

Cube. Make light layers of crosshatched lines with the Micro C tip, and then strengthen them with the C tip in areas that you want darker.

Cone and cylinder. Crosshatch with the C tip. Then, along the edge of the shape itself, strengthen the outline between the shadow and the cone or cylinder.

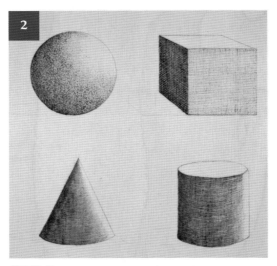

STEP 2. Add shading to the four basic shapes.

ADDING COLOR WITH WATERCOLOR WASHES

As I discussed in the Tools and Materials section, I prefer to use coloring techniques in which the paint remains transparent so that the woodburned lines show clearly through the glaze of color.

I have two favorite media for coloring my woodburnings: watercolors and oil paints. Watercolors provide a convenient way to color your work. All of the projects that require color in this book can be done with watercolors.

I also like to use oil paints thinned to transparency with low-odor mineral spirits to create color washes for my woodburnings. A personal caution: in my own experience, I have learned *not* to use linseed oil media to thin the oil paint on woodburnings. Over time, the linseed oil, if used too thickly, can lift the dark burned wood right out of the woodburned lines. I have had to re-burn several pieces on which I had used linseed oil media to dilute my oil paints. Mineral spirits, used sparingly, work very well as a thinning medium for oil paints.

Always buy the highest quality professional watercolor paints you can afford to assure lightfastness and vibrancy of color. I use the Winsor and Newton Professional Artist's Watercolors, not their Cotman line, which is a student grade of watercolor. But be sure to shop around for the brand that best suits you. I also like the Daniel Smith line of watercolors, which come in many colors not available anywhere else.

HOW TO APPLY WATERCOLOR TO THE CRAZY QUILT SAMPLER

For the Crazy Quilt Sampler project, you will need the following eight colors:

YO—Yellow ochre light. A slightly opaque, gentle, quiet tan-gold, easy to control, very natural looking.

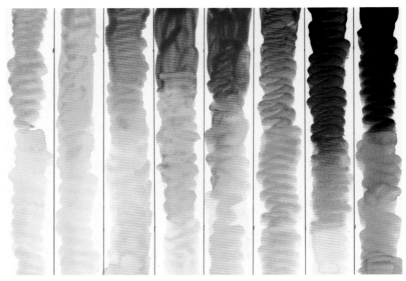

Eight watercolors on white paper. Here you can see the colors as they look against a white background.

RS—Raw sienna. More intensely golden and orange toned than yellow ochre light—radiant and vibrant, very transparent.

BO—Brown ochre. Nice transparent red-brown; a gentle, quiet color.

QG—Quinacridone gold. Very intense staining power; deep yellowish red-gold. Because it has such a difficult name to pronounce, students have nicknamed this color "Quinna-quinna."

BS—Burnt sienna. Very intense staining power; a lovely reddish brown.

RU—Raw umber. A quiet, warm brown, easy to control.

BU—Burnt umber. Warm, beautiful dark brown; high staining power, and somewhat opaque. Be careful not to make the layer of paint too thick or dark or it may obscure the woodburned lines. Very useful color, and can be mixed in combination with Van Dyke brown, to create warm, dark washes. I use this color the most in my woodburnings.

VB—Van Dyke brown. A very dark neutral brown. Again, be careful to thin the paint enough so that the woodburned lines can be clearly seen.

In the illustration on page 64, the colors from left to right are: yellow ochre light, raw sienna, brown ochre, quinacridone gold, burnt sienna, raw umber, burnt umber, and Van Dyke brown.

As you work your way through the projects and develop your woodburning skills, you will probably want to add other colors to your collection. Here are some additional colors that I like to use: cadmium red light, cadmium yellow light, sap green, French ultramarine blue, cerulean blue, quinacridone violet or dioxane purple, and Payne's gray.

Remember, it is the mixtures of these colors that creates subtle effects. For example, a tiny touch of red or burnt sienna into sap green will get rid of the garish bright quality of the green. There are many good books on color mixing at the library or in bookstores and craft shops that can help you produce more natural looking colors for your woodburnings.

The goal in this exercise is to practice creating very dark areas of concentrated color contrasted with very diluted washes, so that you can see the full range that each color is capable of producing. This will give you a reference guide for future projects. Before putting the colors on wood, you may want to make a simple chart on white paper to see how the colors look on a white background, as in the illustration on page 64. This helps show each color's characteristics, which can vary in surprising ways, from the most diluted wash of color to a concentrated dark tone.

SETTING UP YOUR PALETTE

With a permanent marker, label the initials of each of the eight colors on your plastic palette.

Now, with a small "round" brush, (the round brush comes to a point) proceed to fill in the inner circle of your sampler with color. You can apply the watercolor to each triangular "pie-wedge" with any small (size 2, 4, or 6) sable or synthetic watercolor brush. I have chosen not to color the squares of the sampler, which lie outside the inner circle, but you may want to.

I constantly keep a paper towel handy to blot up excess watercolor. If an area of color appears too dark, you can dilute the color with a wet brush or wet paper towel and blot immediately to lift the color from the wood.

You may need to redefine some of the woodburned lines after applying the watercolor wash. Use a hairdryer to completely dry the color wash before reburning. You can also use your scraper as a creative tool to work scraped lines into colored areas to create light fur lines, whiskers, or rays of light from stars.

When you are satisfied with your sampler, sign and date it, using your Micro C tip. Let it dry overnight, and then put on a final finish of your choice. (Please see "Final Finishing" in the Supplies section, page 21.)

Eight watercolors labeled and arranged on a palette.

Chapter 4:
SAW-WHET OWL
STEP-BY-STEP BASIC PROJECT

Owls are one of my favorite subjects to woodburn. I am fascinated by their mysterious and intense expressions and their huge, intelligent eyes. I have chosen the tiny, northern saw-whet owl as my central image. This dainty, beautifully marked owl is the smallest North American owl, weighing about three pounds (1.4kg) and standing 8" (205mm) tall. It is the height of an average American robin.

The saw-whet owl may look small when perched, but in flight it appears larger because of its broad wingspan of 17" (432mm). These owls are strictly nocturnal. During the day, their plumage helps to camouflage them as they roost in deep foliage, usually fairly close to the ground.

THE CENTRAL IMAGE

Referring to the image at right, let's study the saw-whet owl with "artist's eyes."

The saw-whet owl has a large head in relation to its body. Its round, bright golden eyes have enormous black pupils. Unlike the screech owl, the saw-whet has no visible ear tufts. It has fine white stripes on the top of its head, and larger, reddish brown and white stripes on its chest and belly. White spots on the flight feathers on its back and wings add to its appeal.

Notice how the facial disk has brown and white radials around the edge, which fade to a light whitish area around the eyes. There is also a dark area from the base of the bill to the bottom inside edge of each eye. The forehead is densely covered with fine white streaks, which conform to the contours of the head. The bill is black. The plumage is quite fluffy and down-like, and even the legs and feet are heavily covered with light buff-colored feathers. The claws are dark brown horn with blackish tips.

Saw-whet owls like coniferous forests but also live in oak woodland or streamside groves. They look for nesting cavities in trees with abandoned woodpecker holes. I have chosen to put my subject in an oak tree so that I can use the oak leaves, branches, and acorns as motifs in my composition.

Completed saw-whet owl woodburning with watercolor washes.

Detail from the pattern for the saw-whet owl woodburning project. For the full-size pattern, see page 164.

DESIGNING THE PATTERN

To design my pattern, I first traced the exact outline of my wood piece on a large sheet of tracing paper. I did all of my design work on the tracing paper, not on the wood itself.

It can take me several days to plan a design. I like to play with the different elements, percolating ideas, and moving them around. I try out many different arrangements, until all of the elements feel balanced to me.

I have chosen to work on a 16" (406mm) diameter basswood platter that is beaded on the inner circle and scalloped along the outer edge. I will work initially in the central area, which is 9½" (241mm) in diameter. There is a slightly concave scoop along the edge of the central area, where it meets the beaded edge. Later on, I am planning to add a border and a saying to the central image, in steps 2 and 3 of this project.

You can, of course, do this project on any size basswood platter or birch panel, simply by enlarging or reducing the pattern before transferring it. You can either trace the central image pattern on page 164 or scan it into a computer, and then print it at your desired size. Copier machines at libraries or office supply stores can also do these procedures for you.

Using four different photographs of saw-whet owls, I created a composite image, so that I am not exactly copying any one photograph. I also changed the direction of the owl's gaze, enlarged the pupils, and moved the highlights in the eyes to accentuate their startling intensity and make it appear that the owl is staring directly at the viewer, which gives the woodburning more impact.

Then came the really fun part! Carrying a bag and small clippers to collect specimens, I went on a nature walk around my backyard, carefully studying and choosing oak leaves, branches, and acorns. I like to lay out my finds on a board and pick my favorites.

I then sketched, scanned and/or traced these images. I photocopied and reduced or enlarged the images, cut them out, and physically moved them around on the tracing paper until the composition felt right.

This stage can take a long time. I used to get impatient with this phase of the creative process, wanting to get right to the woodburning. I have learned that taking the time to create a satisfying design is vital. Why put in ten, twenty, thirty or more hours of woodburning time into an unbalanced design? You will enjoy the woodburning work much more if you "program for success" with a well thought out composition.

Leaves and acorns chosen as references for the woodburning. On a nature walk around my backyard, I chose oak leaves, branches, and acorns, then laid them on a board and picked my favorites.

My basic pattern on tracing paper with all shapes and elements taped into place, and ready to transfer. After selecting the elements, I sketched, scanned and/or traced them. Then I made reduced or enlarged photocopies of the elements, cut them out, and physically moved them around on the tracing paper until the composition felt right.

WOODBURNING THE CENTRAL IMAGE

Choose a wood piece, and prepare the surface by sanding, either by hand, or with the random orbit sander (see page 18).

After studying the grain pattern of your wood, tape the pattern to the wood, and transfer it with graphite transfer paper.

After transferring the pattern, use a (warmed-up) kneaded eraser to gently lighten all the graphite lines, carefully removing any smudges accidentally left on the wood.

STEP 1: WOODBURNING THE EYES

I find it helpful to burn the darkest areas of a composition first. Once the deepest tones have been established, it is easier to judge how dark to make all the other tones, from medium to light.

Perhaps you have heard the quote, "The eyes are the windows of the soul." Let's make the owl's eyes as striking and dramatic as we can, since the eyes should be the magnetic center of interest—the focal point—of the whole composition.

Artists know the viewer's eye will always be drawn to the area in a picture with the darkest darks and the lightest lights. Extreme value contrast creates drama and interest. Let's use this artistic concept to our advantage with the owl's eyes. Remember to first practice your strokes on scrap wood.

First, lightly outline the pupil and the dark ring around the eyes with your C tip. We can always get darker, so start with light, tentative strokes and gradually darken them. Rest the palm of your hand on a lint-free cloth as you

Transferred pattern with eyes woodburned. After studying the grain pattern of your wood, tape the pattern to the wood, and transfer it with graphite transfer paper.

work so as not to smudge the graphite outlines under your hand.

Burning in a neat circle can be tricky—work in short strokes, always remembering to turn the wood so you can keep pulling the tip toward you, as you create overlapping curved strokes.

We also need to outline the outer circle of the eye. Using the wide, flat edge of the Mini J tip, fill in the black pupil. Then, with the sharp edge of the Mini J tip, darken the outer dark ring around the eye. The edge of the outer dark ring will need to transition into feathers, so keep the outer edge soft, not a hard outline.

The highlight in the eye can be left as bare, unburned wood, or scraped out with a blade if you accidentally burn it. Using the flat, curved edge of the S tip, fill in the iris with light golden tones. Start at a very low heat setting with the shader so as not to make too dark a mark, and gradually increase the temperature to achieve the tone you desire. Try to curve your strokes to express the rounded shape of the eyeball. I have also shaded a bit darker across the top of the eyeball to suggest the shadow cast by the top eyelid.

Using the Mini J tip, now outline and fill in the beak and talons, leaving a highlight on each talon. Indicate feathering along the edges of the beak. We will go back later to redefine the eyes even more, but we now have a good start and a sense of the spunky personality of our little owl.

STEP 2: OUTLINE LEAVES, BRANCHES, AND MOON

In preparation for shading the central image's background, we need to outline the leaves, branches, twigs, and moon. I used the sharp, curved edge of the Mini J tip for this, but you can also use the C tip. I prefer the lighter line that the Mini J tip makes to the bolder C line in these beginning stages, but experiment and use whichever is more comfortable for you. Remember to keep turning the wood so you pull the tip toward you with each stroke. (I cannot emphasize this enough, since it will give you much greater control.)

Make the outline around the moon a very light line because the night sky shading we'll do in the area adjacent to the moon will be lighter in the area closest to the moon. The leaf outlines can be darker. I have also woodburned the main leaf veins within each leaf and lightly indicated where the owl's body meets the sky, near the wings and feet. You do not want to make a hard outline around the owl's body—that would look unnatural. We want to create a soft edge where the fluffy feathers meet the dark shading of the sky. Keep this area rather ambiguous for now—we'll sharpen it up when we woodburn the owl's feathers in step 5.

When the outlining is complete, erase any graphite guidelines in the leaves and moon with your kneaded eraser.

STEP 1. Woodburn the eyes by working in short strokes, turning the wood and pulling the tip toward you as you create overlapping curved strokes.

STEP 2. Use the curved edge of the Mini J tip to outline the leaves, branches, twigs, and moon.

STEP 3: SHADING THE CENTRAL IMAGE'S NIGHT SKY BACKGROUND

Let's shade the background to create the effect of a night sky and also to establish our darkest darks in the background area.

With the flat, curved area of the S tip, move in small, circular motions to create the burled wood effect that we used on the Crazy Quilt Sampler border (page 53). Start with a low heat setting and slowly build up the temperature to achieve the desired level of darkness. Different areas of the wood may need lower or higher settings to burn to the same tone. To get into tight areas, such as between the leaf lobes, flip the S tip over and use the point upside-down. Scrape away any errors on stems or branches with your knife or gently rub with 220-grit sandpaper. Don't worry about an uneven mottled appearance—this will only add to the rustic, natural look.

STEP 4: OWL FACE

It is amazing how many different shapes of feathers can appear on one little bird. The entire head was done with the Mini J tip. Don't rush. Let the lines build up slowly. Follow the guidelines for direction of strokes in the illustration on page 73.

We want the owl's body and feathers to stand out against the dark background, so all of our texturing of feathers must remain somewhat lighter than the background. Because the feathers on the head of the owl are very small, it's not necessary to make each feather extremely detailed. We can simply suggest the central quill of each feather, if it shows at all, with a single, rather than double burned line. Remember to curve the lines of the feather vanes coming from the quill. We can convey an impression of feathers without delineating every single feather. The feathers at the top and far sides of the head are smooth and dark with white dashes and do not need a lot of detail. Using the Mini J tip on its sharp, curved edge, pull the strokes from the top of the head toward the center of the face, leaving light dashes of unburned wood. You can also scrape out the dashes with your knife after burning. Turn the wood as you work. After establishing the light and dark areas, turn the Mini J on its side and stroke in some soft shading to blend and soften the dark areas.

The light, circular ruffs around the owl's eyes will blend into the dark parts above and to the sides. Curve these lines, drawing the Mini J tip from the dark outline around the eyes outward toward the darker feathers. Use the flat edge of the Mini J for a softer look, or the sharp edge for clear, detailed lines.

Notice the three rows of short horizontal dashes on each side below the beak. Beneath these are rows of C-shaped crescents that create a ruffled effect between the head and body. When we work on the body in step 5, we'll concentrate more on this area.

STEP 3. Use the flat, curved area of the S tip to shade in the darkness of the night sky background of the central image.

Owl face directional arrows woodburning chart.

STEP 4. Pull the strokes from the top of the head toward the center of the face, leaving light dashes of unburned wood. Turn the wood as you work. After establishing the light and dark areas, stroke in some soft shading to blend and soften the dark areas.

To define the head and separate it from the background, darken the edge of the head on the left side where it touches the lighter moonlit sky. The right side of the head needs to remain light to separate it from the dark night sky.

STEP 5: THE OWL'S BODY

The saw-whet owl depends on its plumage for camouflage during the daytime when it roosts in foliage. Mother Nature has certainly done a marvelous job of creating an effect of dappled light on its feathers to help hide it from predators.

There are three main types of feathers to woodburn in the body: feathers with quills and vanes, overlapping body feathers, and wing feathers. Please refer to the illustration on page 74 for help with the direction of strokes for the three types of feathers.

Feathers with central quills and vanes. These feathers are found on the lower parts of the wings on the left and right sides of the owl. Use the Mini J tip on its sharp, curved edge to first burn the central curved line of the quills. Then, pulling from the quill toward you, make the shorter, curved lines of the vanes. Do

STEP 5. First burn the central curved line of the quills. Then, pulling from the quill toward you, make the shorter, curved lines of the vanes. Do not outline the edges of these feathers, which would make them look unnatural and stiff.

not outline the edges of these feathers, which would make them look unnatural and stiff.

To create a realistic edge, use the S tip to shade the area of dark sky behind the wings on the left. Then use your scraper knife to etch out curved light feather vanes into the dark area of the sky. Do the same on the lower right.

Overlapping body feathers. These are soft, fluffy feathers that overlap in clumps. Use the Mini J on its sharp, curved edge. Curve the strokes in the direction shown in the chart.

Wing feathers. These have white dots and white bars along their edges. Leave the lightest feather areas and dots as bare wood with just a few light, wispy lines to indicate some texturing.

By scraping with your knife, you can lighten areas that you would like to highlight in the overlapping feathers and wing feathers. This will give your work a more textured and three-dimensional appearance.

There is a delicate ruff of short feathers between the head and body. Indicate this with overlapped crescent-shaped strokes, and scrape out between them if necessary to create a light/dark pattern around the neck, separating it from the body.

Let's complete the leaves and branches in the central image, and then we'll go back and refine the owl's feet and the branch on which he is perched.

Owl body directional arrows woodburning chart.

STEP 6. It is important that you not allow the leaves and branches in the central image to become too dark in tone. They create a balanced composition and provide dramatic value contrast to the dark sky. If all the elements are too dark, the picture looks murky and lifeless.

STEP 6: CENTRAL IMAGE LEAVES AND BRANCHES

Although you must realistically texture the leaves and branches in the central image, it is of utmost importance that you do not allow them to become too dark in tone. The light leaves and branches in the central image create a balanced composition and provide dramatic value contrast to the dark sky. If all the elements become too dark, the picture looks murky and lifeless.

Leaves. Using the curved, sharp edge of the Mini J tip on a low-heat setting, lightly indicate the veins in the leaves, and add some light shading with curved parallel contour lines. The sections of the leaves within the circle of the moon can be a bit darker, since they will show up nicely against the light moon.

Now use the wide flat edge of the Mini J tip to shade darkly on the outside of the leaf outline, especially between the lobes of the leaves.

This will make the leaf stand out clearly from the background and the owl's body.

Oak branch. The bark on the tree branch is composed of distinctive cracks that deepen as the oak tree ages. For design inspiration for the tree branch, I decided to go right to the source—Mother Nature. I went outside and studied the bark of the huge oak tree in our backyard and brought in a few fallen branches to help me create realistic detail. I worked out my design for the branch on the tracing paper pattern, and then transferred it to the wood.

Leaf directional arrows woodburning chart.

First, I used the sharp edge of the Mini J tip to portray the cracked, deep line patterns of the bark. You could also use the C or Micro C tip if you prefer. I then added the appearance of holes bored by insects with the C tip. The wide, flat edge of the Mini J or the S tip can be used to shade and create even more texture effects and to darken areas under and between the deep cracks.

STEP 7: FEATHERED FEET ON THE OWL

Once the tree branch is complete, add more curved feathers to the claws so they don't look like fingers! You can then scrape light "feathers" between the darker burned lines to soften the edge between the feet and claws and the tree branch.

STEP 7. Add curved feathers to the claws so they don't look like fingers. Scrape light "feathers" between the darker burned lines to soften the edge between the feet and claws and the tree branch.

THE BORDER AND OPTIONAL SAYING

STEP 1: OUTLINING THE BORDER LEAVES

Notice that the leaves in the border area will be larger and darker than those in the central image and that the background in the border will be much lighter than the night sky in the central image. Begin by woodburning the outlines of all of the leaves, and lightly indicate the main leaf veins using the sharp edge of the Mini J tip. Use your kneaded eraser to remove residual graphite lines after burning the outlines.

As I work, I always find it helpful to have real leaves on my work table for reference. Don't be afraid to add their unique irregularities and imperfections. A torn edge, a hole, or oddly shaped lobe creates realism in your work.

STEP 2: SHADING THE BORDER LEAVES

As in the central image, use the Mini J's sharp edge to build up the vein patterns within the leaves, and shade with parallel curved contour lines. Over these lines, you can shade with the flat surface of the Mini J or with the S tip, to add depth. Darken and thicken the leaf outline within the leaf lobes and along parts of the

Pattern for border. For the complete pattern, see page 164.

Twelve leaves chosen for the border area. Taped and numbered for reference while working.

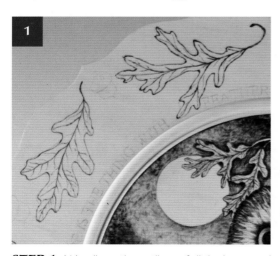

STEP 1. Woodburn the outlines of all the leaves and lightly indicate the main leaf veins using the sharp edge of the Mini J tip. Use your kneaded eraser to remove residual graphite lines after burning the outlines.

STEP 2. Build up the vein patterns within the leaves and shade them with parallel curved contour lines. Over these lines, shade with the flat surface of the Mini J or with the S tip to add depth.

STEP 3. Outline the acorn with the sharp edge of the Mini J tip. Then make the pattern on the acorn's cap with curved lines. Darken the lower parts of the criss-cross lines as they curve around the lower edge of the cap. Then, darken the outline between the cap and the acorn.

STEP 4. Gently shade and texture the background of the border to tie all of the elements together. Leave a ⅛" (3mm) border of bare wood around each leaf and acorn so that it stands out against the background. To add words in the next step, leave this area blank for now. Make a thin dark burned line along the outer scalloped edge of the wood for a subtle finished look to the piece.

curves on leaf edges. Make sure the central leaf vein and the veins radiating from it to the ends of each leaf lobe show up clearly and strongly within the shading lines.

STEP 3: WOODBURNING THE BORDER ACORNS

The acorns provide a balance and a design counterpoint to the owl's eyes. They are about the same size as the eyes, and I have made them very detailed and dark with bright highlights, just like the eyes.

In the illustration at left, you can see the acorns in various stages. First, outline the acorn with the sharp edge of the Mini J tip. Then, make the diagonal, criss-cross pattern on the acorn's cap with curved lines, not straight, since the lines curve around the cap. The directional arrows chart in the illustration at left shows the direction to move your woodburning tip as you burn. Using the Mini J tip's sharp edge, darken the lower parts of the criss-cross lines as they curve around the lower edge of the cap. Then, darken the outline between the cap and the acorn.

With the Mini J edge, or the Micro C tip, draw the stems. For interest, bend the stem of each acorn in a different direction.

Border acorns directional arrows woodburning chart.

Using the wide, flat edge of the Mini J tip, pull broad strokes of shading horizontally across the acorn. To create a three-dimensional rounded effect, make the outlined edges of the acorn darker and leave highlights (the highlights are bare wood) in the central area of the acorn.

Make a dark shadow beneath the cap to show its cast shadow on the acorn. In the bottom area of the border there are empty acorn caps. Shade inside these with the flat edge of the Mini J or the S tip, and make the small inner circle inside the cap very dark. Make the curved criss-cross pattern on the outside of these caps. Shade with curved diagonal lines inside the cap to create roundness.

STEP 4: SHADING THE BORDER BACKGROUND

The next step is to gently shade and texture the background of the border to tie all of the elements together. Using the rounded curve of the S tip, create the "burled wood effect" that we used for the night sky in the central image, but keep the tone much lighter.

Move the tip in small, circular motions. Leave a ⅛-inch (3mm) border of bare wood around each leaf and acorn so that it stands out against the background. Because I am planning to add words to my border in the next step, I will leave this area blank for now.

Make a thin dark burned line along the outer scalloped edge of the wood to give a subtle finished look to the piece.

STEP 5: SHADE THE LEAVES

Once the border background is textured, you can do some shading on the leaves in the border. Use the rounded surface of the S tip to shade over the woodburned lines in the leaves so that they stand out clearly against the background and look three-dimensional. If necessary, use the edge of the rounded point of the S tip to redefine the leaf veins so they don't get lost in the shading. The outsides and insides of the acorn caps can also be shaded slightly.

At this point, you can also touch up the central image leaves, with just a small amount of shading. Remember, it's important that these leaves remain *lighter* than the background in the central image.

STEP 6: FINISHING TOUCHES

Don't forget to sign your name with your Micro C tip. Practice your signature on a piece of scrap wood. You can put the signature anywhere on the woodburning. I also like to include the year that I made the piece.

Burnt umber wash of watercolor. I usually prefer a natural, monochromatic look in my work that showcases the simple beauty of the wood itself and the burned lines and textures. I feel pleased with the variety of burned tones and textures in this woodburning, so I have decided to add only burnt umber watercolor washes to it. As you work at applying the diluted burnt

ADDING A SAYING TO YOUR WOODBURNING

If you prefer not to add a saying to your woodburning, you can simply shade lightly all the way to the bare wood ring that separates the central image from the border.

It is easy to add lettering to your woodburnings without having to learn calligraphy. Simply print out the saying you have chosen on the computer, trying various fonts and sizes. Some of my favorite fonts are Times New Roman, Bookman Old Style, Cambria, Monotype Corsiva, and Lucida Handwriting. It's fun to see how the words change as each font is applied. Decide if you want to use uppercase or lowercase lettering. Then print out the saying in various font sizes, depending on the size of your project.

The next step is to draw ruled lines beneath and above the letters, and cut them out in strips. Most of my projects are rounded; it is easy to form the letters into curves by partially clipping between the words and letters and then physically bending the paper. Tape the curved lettering to the pattern. If you are a whiz at the computer, this curving process can actually be done on the computer, but I find it much easier to do by hand.

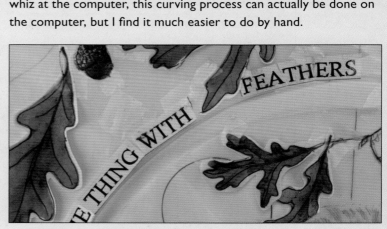
Curved lettering on tracing paper pattern (close-up).

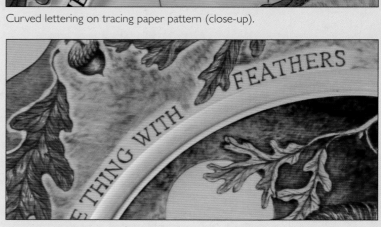
Woodburned lettering with shading blended around letters.

umber paint to the woodburning, use a paper towel to blot and rub the washes while they are still damp to soften the edges and transitions.

If you prefer the look of color, you could add lovely autumn colors to the leaves and to the owl's feathers. The eyes would look startling with light golden washes of color. Remember not to put color in the highlight area in the eye so that it remains light. Keep the washes transparent so that the beautiful burned lines you have worked so hard to create remain clearly visible through the color. You may need to lightly reburn some lines to redefine them after the watercolor has dried.

You can see the finished woodburning, with the burnt umber watercolor wash applied in the photograph below.

In order to preserve the very lightest tones of the bare wood, I have decided not to use the thirds mixture to finish this particular piece because it might darken the highlights too much. I have simply sprayed on a couple of light coats of semi-gloss polyurethane to protect the wood.

I hope you are pleased with your saw-whet owl! Whoooo knewwww that yooouuuu could create such a charming little fellow so easily?

STEPS 5 AND 6.
Once the border background is textured, shade the leaves in the border, the outsides and insides of the acorn caps, and you can also touch up the central image leaves with just a small amount of shading. Other finishing touches include your signature, a watercolor wash, and several light coats of spray-on polyurethane to preserve the wood.

Chapter 5:
PATTERN TREASURY

Elements patterns can be used in many versatile ways. Several elements patterns can be combined to create a border design. Or, if you prefer a less busy look, a single element pattern can be enlarged and used as a central image, without a border. You could also use a single element to create a small vignette that could stand alone as a simple design to adorn a wooden box, mirror frame, decorative cutting board, or platter. Note that all the pieces shown in this section were done on either basswood platters or birch panels, which are readily available in craft stores or through online sources.

ELEMENTS
FLOWERS, PLANTS, AND TREES

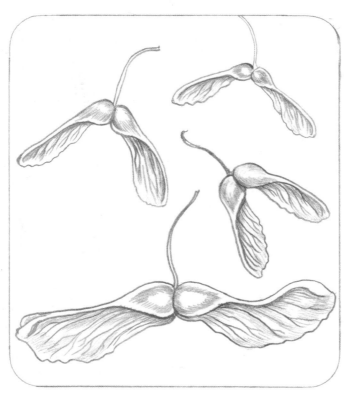
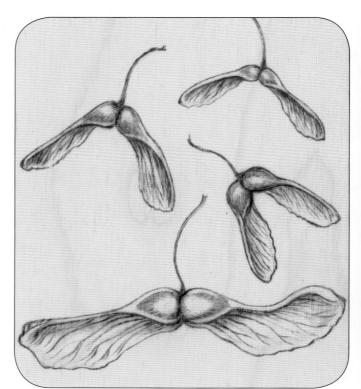

Maple and sycamore winged seedpods.

ELEMENTS
FLOWERS, PLANTS, AND TREES *(CONTINUED)*

Pine cones and needles on branch.

Dogwood blossoms, leaves, and berries.

ELEMENTS
FLOWERS, PLANTS, AND TREES (CONTINUED)

Rose.

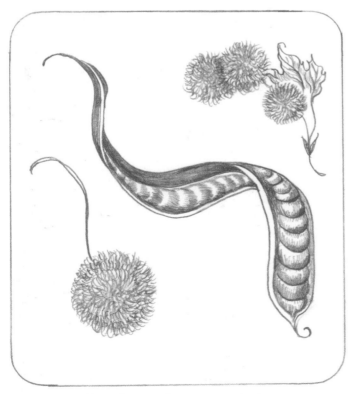

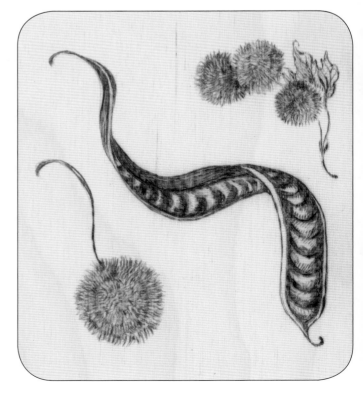

Honey locust and sycamore seedpods.

ELEMENTS
FLOWERS, PLANTS, AND TREES *(CONTINUED)*

Ferns.

Thistles.

ELEMENTS
FLOWERS, PLANTS, AND TREES (CONTINUED)

Oak leaf.

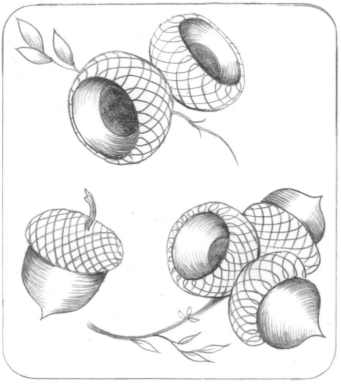

Acorns.

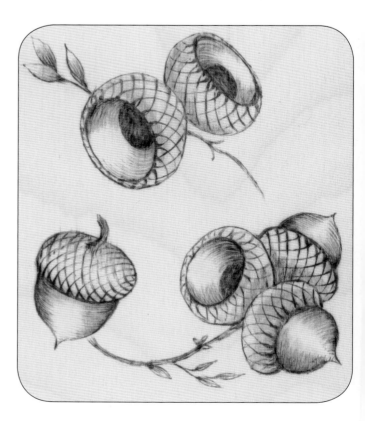

ELEMENTS
FLOWERS, PLANTS, AND TREES *(CONTINUED)*

Bleeding hearts flowers and leaves.

Morning glories.

ELEMENTS
FLOWERS, PLANTS, AND TREES (CONTINUED)

Pumpkins and gourds.

Indian corn.

ELEMENTS
BIRDS

Blue jay design 1.

Blue jay design 2.

OTHER SIMILARLY THEMED PATTERNS
Complete compositions:

- Kind Hearts are Gardens, page 116
- I'll Put a Trinket On, page 136
- Simple Gifts, page 138
- To Everything There Is a Season, page 152
- Dreamcatcher, page 104
- Small Things with Great Love, page 132
- Ode to Joy, page 160

ELEMENTS
BIRDS *(CONTINUED)*

Bird's nest with eggs.

Flying birds.

ELEMENTS
BIRDS *(CONTINUED)*

Feather design 1.

Feather design 2.

Feather design 3.

ELEMENTS
CELTIC KNOT WORK

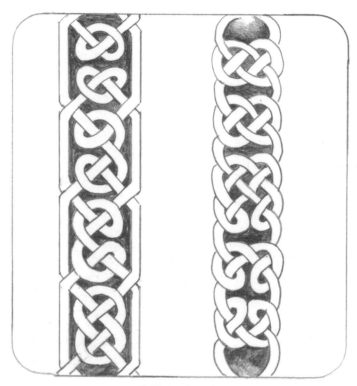

Celtic knot work.

ELEMENTS
SEWING AND COOKING

OTHER SIMILARLY THEMED PATTERNS
Complete compositions:
- Young at Heart, page 118
- Tea Time, page 110
- In Thine Ocean Depths, page 150

Sewing machine.

ELEMENTS
SEWING AND COOKING *(CONTINUED)*

Thimbles and thread.

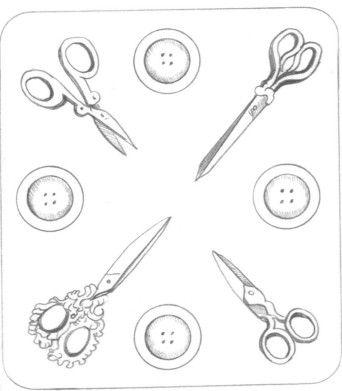

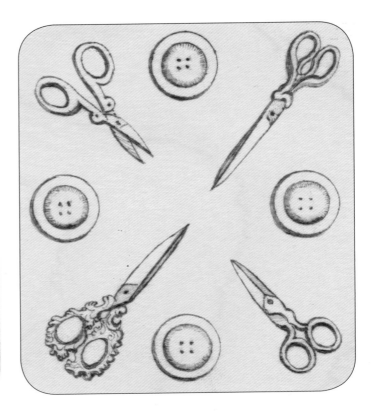

Scissors and buttons.

ELEMENTS
SEWING AND COOKING *(CONTINUED)*

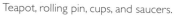
Teapot, rolling pin, cups, and saucers.

ELEMENTS
ANIMALS AND INSECTS

Horses design 1.

OTHER SIMILARLY THEMED PATTERNS
Complete compositions:

- Until They Rest In You, page 156
- Dreamcatcher, page 104
- The Loveliest of All Was the Unicorn, page 106
- Simple Gifts, page 138
- Ode to Joy, page 160

Horses design 2.

ELEMENTS
ANIMALS AND INSECTS (CONTINUED)

Butterflies design 1.

Butterflies design 2.

ELEMENTS
ANIMALS AND INSECTS *(CONTINUED)*

Swan.

Five turtles on a log with wild strawberries. Enlarge pattern 150% for actual size. For woodburning shading reference, see page 161.

ELEMENTS
ANIMALS AND INSECTS *(CONTINUED)*

Watering can with flying warbler. Enlarge pattern 150% for actual size.

ELEMENTS
ANIMALS AND INSECTS *(CONTINUED)*

Rabbit in clover with daffodils. Enlarge pattern 150% for actual size.

ELEMENTS
THE SEA

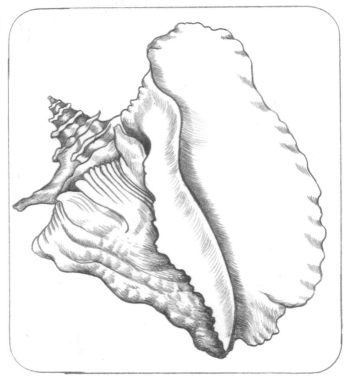

Conch shell.

OTHER SIMILARLY THEMED PATTERNS
Complete compositions:
- By the Sea, page 108
- In Thine Ocean Depths, page 150
- Until They Rest in You, page 156

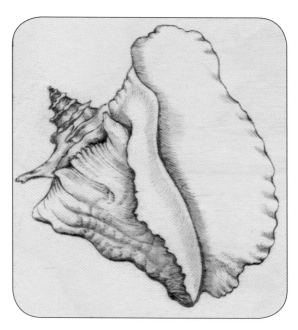

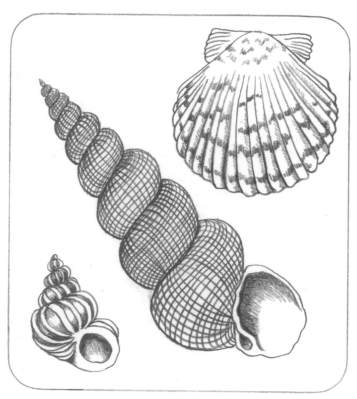

Sea shells.

ELEMENTS
THE SEA (CONTINUED)

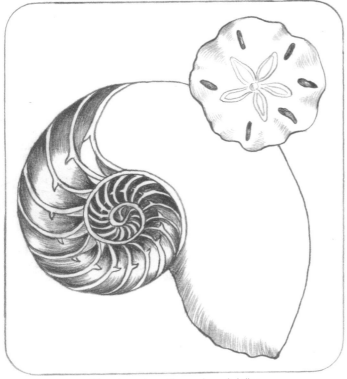

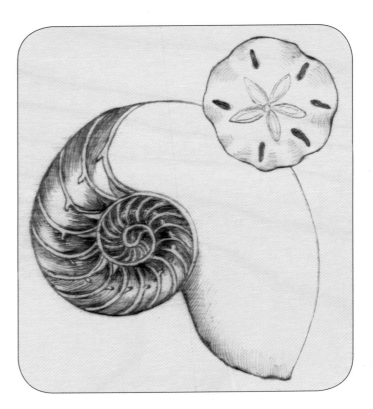

Chambered nautilus and sand dollar.

Sea gulls.

COMPLETE COMPOSITIONS
BEGINNER- AND INTERMEDIATE-LEVEL PATTERNS

"Munchkin and Freckles."

COMPLETE COMPOSITIONS
BEGINNER- AND INTERMEDIATE-LEVEL PATTERNS

"Dreamcatcher."

COMPLETE COMPOSITIONS
BEGINNER- AND INTERMEDIATE-LEVEL PATTERNS

"The Loveliest of All Was the Unicorn."

OTHER SIMILARLY THEMED PATTERNS

Elements:

- Rose, page 84
- Butterflies design 1 and 2, page 96
- Swan, page 97

COMPLETE COMPOSITIONS
BEGINNER- AND INTERMEDIATE-LEVEL PATTERNS

"By the Sea."

OTHER SIMILARLY THEMED PATTERNS

Elements:

- Conch shell, page 100
- Sea shells, page 100
- Chambered nautilus and sand dollar, page 101
- Sea gulls, page 101

COMPLETE COMPOSITIONS
BEGINNER- AND INTERMEDIATE-LEVEL PATTERNS

"Tea Time."

OTHER SIMILARLY THEMED PATTERNS
Elements:
- Teapot, rolling pin, cups, and saucers, page 94

COMPLETE COMPOSITIONS
BEGINNER- AND INTERMEDIATE-LEVEL PATTERNS

"A Little Nut."

THE MIGHTIEST OAK WAS ONCE A LITTLE NUT THAT HELD ITS GROUND

Pompatio 2008

OTHER SIMILARLY THEMED PATTERNS

Elements:

- Maple and sycamore winged seedpods, page 82
- Pinecones and needles on branch, page 83
- Honey locust and sycamore seedpods, page 84
- Ferns, page 85
- Acorns, page 86
- Pumpkins and gourds, page 88
- Indian corn, page 88

Complete compositions:

- Squirrel Nutkin, page 134
- Autumn Bounty, page 146

COMPLETE COMPOSITIONS
BEGINNER- AND INTERMEDIATE-LEVEL PATTERNS

"Forest Green."

God's Little Creatures of the World
I Love
That Live in the Forest Green

OTHER SIMILARLY THEMED PATTERNS
Elements:
- Morning glories, page 87
- Butterfly designs 1 and 2, page 96

COMPLETE COMPOSITIONS
BEGINNER- AND INTERMEDIATE-LEVEL PATTERNS

"Kind Hearts are Gardens."

The plate illustration reads: "Kind Hearts are Gardens, Kind Thoughts are Roots, Kind Words are Flowers, Kind Deeds are Fruits"

Pompano '09

OTHER SIMILARLY THEMED PATTERNS

Elements:
- Thistles, page 85
- Bird's nest with eggs, page 90
- Flying birds, page 90
- Feather designs 1, 2, and 3, page 91

Complete compositions:
- Kind Hearts are Gardens, page 116

COMPLETE COMPOSITIONS
BEGINNER- AND INTERMEDIATE-LEVEL PATTERNS

"Young at Heart."

OTHER SIMILARLY THEMED PATTERNS

Elements:

- Sewing machine, page 92
- Thimbles and thread, page 93
- Scissors and buttons, page 93

Complete compositions:

- Hands To Work, Hearts To God, page 120

COMPLETE COMPOSITIONS
BEGINNER- AND INTERMEDIATE-LEVEL PATTERNS

"Hands to Work, Hearts to God."

OTHER SIMILARLY THEMED PATTERNS

Elements:
- Sewing machine, page 92
- Thimbles and thread, page 93
- Scissors and buttons, page 93

Complete compositions:
- Young At Heart, page 118

COMPLETE COMPOSITIONS
BEGINNER- AND INTERMEDIATE-LEVEL PATTERNS

"A Mother's Love."

COMPLETE COMPOSITIONS
BEGINNER- AND INTERMEDIATE-LEVEL PATTERNS

"What Happened?"

Some people make things happen, Some people watch things happen, And some people wonder "What happened?"

Pompano 2009

Photographic reference for the chimpanzee by Michael Turco © 2009.

COMPLETE COMPOSITIONS
BEGINNER- AND INTERMEDIATE-LEVEL PATTERNS

"Moe, Larry, and Curly."

OTHER SIMILARLY THEMED PATTERNS
Elements:
- Dogwood blossoms, leaves, and berries (added to border), page 83

COMPLETE COMPOSITIONS
BEGINNER- AND INTERMEDIATE-LEVEL PATTERNS

"All Things Wise and Wonderful."

ALL THINGS BRIGHT AND BEAUTIFUL, ALL CREATURES GREAT AND SMALL, ALL THINGS WISE AND WONDERFUL, THE LORD GOD MADE THEM ALL.

OTHER SIMILARLY THEMED PATTERNS
Elements:
- Pinecones and needles on branch, page 83
- Feather designs 1, 2, and 3, page 91

COMPLETE COMPOSITIONS
BEGINNER- AND INTERMEDIATE-LEVEL PATTERNS

"He Made Their Tiny Wings."

OTHER SIMILARLY THEMED PATTERNS
Elements:
- Morning glories, page 87

COMPLETE COMPOSITIONS
BEGINNER- AND INTERMEDIATE-LEVEL PATTERNS

"Small Things with Great Love."

OTHER SIMILARLY THEMED PATTERNS

Elements:

- Bleeding hearts flowers and leaves, page 87
- Flying birds, page 90
- Feather designs 1, 2, and 3, page 91

COMPLETE COMPOSITIONS
BEGINNER- AND INTERMEDIATE-LEVEL PATTERNS

"Squirrel Nutkin."

OTHER SIMILARLY THEMED PATTERNS

Elements:

- Maple and sycamore winged seedpods, page 82
- Pinecones and needles on branch, page 83
- Honey locust and sycamore seedpods, page 84
- Ferns, page 85
- Oak leaf, page 86
- Acorns, page 86
- Pumpkins and gourds, page 88
- Indian corn, page 88

Complete compositions:

- A Little Nut, page 112

COMPLETE COMPOSITIONS
BEGINNER- AND INTERMEDIATE-LEVEL PATTERNS

"I'll Put a Trinket On."

The morns are meeker than they were, the nuts are getting brown, the berry's cheek is plumper, the rose is out of town. The maple wears a gayer scarf, the field a scarlet gown, Lest I should be old-fashioned, I'll put a trinket on. Emily Dickinson

Deborah Pompano 2007

OTHER SIMILARLY THEMED PATTERNS
Elements:
- Pumpkins and gourds, page 88
- Indian corn, page 88
- Bird's nests with eggs, page 90

COMPLETE COMPOSITIONS
BEGINNER- AND INTERMEDIATE-LEVEL PATTERNS

"Simple Gifts."

The image reads around the border: "'Tis a gift to be simple, 'Tis a gift to be free, 'Tis a gift to come down where we ought to be, And when we find ourselves in the place just right, We'll be in the garden of love and delight."

OTHER SIMILARLY THEMED PATTERNS

Elements:

- Dogwood blossoms, leaves, and berries, page 83
- Bird's nests with eggs, page 90
- Blue jay designs 1 and 2, page 89
- Butterflies (instead of birds in border), page 96
- Flying birds (use smaller birds), page 90
- Feather designs 1, 2, and 3, page 91

COMPLETE COMPOSITIONS
BEGINNER- AND INTERMEDIATE-LEVEL PATTERNS

"A Special Love."

A MOTHER'S LOVE IS A SPECIAL LOVE THAT LASTS FOREVER

OTHER SIMILARLY THEMED PATTERNS
Elements:
- Rose, page 84
- Morning glories (intertwined with or substituted for roses), page 87

COMPLETE COMPOSITIONS
ADVANCED PATTERNS

"Peace." Enlarge pattern 110% for actual size.

Lord, make me an instrument of your peace, where there is hatred, let me sow love; where there is injury, pardon; where there is darkness, light. Where there is despair, hope; where there is sadness, joy; where there is darkness, light.

COMPLETE COMPOSITIONS
ADVANCED PATTERNS

"Tyger, Tyger Burning Bright." Enlarge pattern 115% for actual size.

COMPLETE COMPOSITIONS
ADVANCED PATTERNS

Earth's crammed with heaven,
And every common bush
Afire with God.

"Autumn Bounty." Enlarge pattern 115% for actual size.

Earth's crammed with heaven,
And every common bush
Afire with God.

Elizabeth Barrett Browning

COMPLETE COMPOSITIONS
ADVANCED PATTERNS

"Only God Can Make a Tree." Enlarge pattern 110% for actual size.

I think that I shall never see
A poem lovely as a tree.

OTHER SIMILARLY THEMED PATTERNS

Elements:

- Pinecones and needles on branch, page 83
- Maple and sycamore winged seedpods, page 82
- Honey locust and sycamore seedpods, page 84
- Oak leaf, page 86
- Acorns, page 86

Complete compositions:

- Autumn Bounty, page 146

COMPLETE COMPOSITIONS
ADVANCED PATTERNS

"In Thine Ocean Depths." Enlarge pattern 110% for actual size.

OTHER SIMILARLY THEMED PATTERNS

Elements:

- Celtic knot work, page 92
- Conch shell (as corner vignette in border), page 100
- Sea shells (corner border vignette), page 100
- Chambered nautilus and sand dollar (corner border vignette), page 101

Complete compositions:

- By the Sea, page 108

COMPLETE COMPOSITIONS
ADVANCED PATTERNS

"To Everything There Is a Season." Enlarge pattern 110% for actual size.

OTHER SIMILARLY THEMED PATTERNS

Elements:

- Dogwood blossoms, leaves, and berries, page 83
- Bird's nests with eggs, page 90
- Flying birds (smaller birds only), page 90

COMPLETE COMPOSITIONS
ADVANCED PATTERNS

"My Soul Longs for You." Enlarge pattern 110% for actual size.

As a deer longs for running streams, so my soul longs for thee, O Lord.

DEBORAH ESTHER POMPANO 2004

Photographic reference for two foreground deer by Daniel J. Cox/Natural Exposures.com.

COMPLETE COMPOSITIONS
ADVANCED PATTERNS

"Until They Rest in You." Enlarge pattern 115% for actual size.

OTHER SIMILARLY THEMED PATTERNS

Elements:

- Horse design 1 and 2, page 95
- Conch shell (for corner vignette), page 100
- Sea shells, page 100
- Chambered nautilus shell and sand dollar, page 101

COMPLETE COMPOSITIONS
ADVANCED PATTERNS

"The Little Chap Who Follows Me." Enlarge pattern 110% for actual size.

I cannot once escape his eyes,
Whate'er he sees me do, he tries—Like me, he says, he's going to be,
The little chap who follows me.
A careful man I ought to be; A little fellow follows me;
DEBORAH ESTHER POMPANO 2007

Excerpt from the poem "A Little Fellow Follows Me," written by Rev. Claude Wisdom White, Sr.

COMPLETE COMPOSITIONS
ADVANCED PATTERNS

"Ode to Joy." Enlarge pattern 110% for actual size.

OTHER SIMILARLY THEMED PATTERNS

Elements:

COMPLETE COMPOSITIONS
ADVANCED PATTERNS

"Pleasant Dreams." Enlarge pattern 125% for actual size.

COMPLETE COMPOSITIONS
ADVANCED PATTERNS

"Hope Is the Thing with Feathers."
See Saw-whet Owl Step-by-Step
Project on page 66.

Hope is the thing with feathers that perches in the soul, and sings the tune without the words, and never stops at all.

OTHER SIMILARLY THEMED PATTERNS
Elements:
- Maple and sycamore winged seedpods, page 82
- Honey locust and sycamore seedpods, page 84
- Oak leaf, page 86
- Acorns, page 86
- Feather designs 1, 2, and 3, page 91

Chapter 6:
GALLERY

Most of the woodburnings in this section are drawn from scenes or people in my own life. Because they are either too complex in design, or too personal, to translate into general patterns, I have put them into the gallery section. I hope you will enjoy looking at them and reading the comments.

This majestic, huge old oak tree sits on a hill in my backyard, and behind it is a neighbor's house. I sat outdoors in early spring near the arbor and the dogwood tree in the foreground and did this woodburning from life. I had to rush to finish the oak tree's small branches before the new leaves hid them from view. It was a great joy to work outdoors listening to the birds and feeling the warm breezes. The beautiful poem by Esther Wood expresses the awe I felt as I studied the miraculous beauty of nature.

This is a portrait of my son-in-law, Drew, who is a talented jazz guitarist. The fretwork and straight lines of the guitar strings were quite a challenge to do in a woodburning. I've heard many people exclaim when they hear that someone is an artist, "Gosh, I can't draw a straight line!" Well, I can tell you that drawing a straight line is not easy for an artist either.

When I was a child, my mother told me that if I listened carefully, I could hear the sound of the ocean inside a conch shell. I photographed a friend of my daughters many years ago as the model for this picture, which symbolizes for me the dreamy, reflective, inner listening and watching for all that is meaningful and beautiful in life.

This is a portrait of my husband's tiny Maltese, Snow Bear, a little eight-pound fellow with a lot of personality. Snow Bear likes to grab my dog Corky's ball and hold it for ransom until he gets a treat. He could care less about playing ball; his whole interest is in the reward! We get a kick out of how smart he is to have figured this out. It was a challenge to take a good photo of him holding the ball, and to keep his white coat looking light while still showing the textures in his fur. Making the background dark created enough value contrast to make the coat appear light against it.

I really enjoyed creating the textures in this woodburning, particularly in the braid. The smooth skin tones were created primarily with color washes carefully applied, blotted and rubbed to create soft gradations. Overuse of lines in the skin tones would have looked harsh. I had to sand off and completely reburn the baby's arm and sleeve, where I had made some serious drawing errors. A drastic remedy, and quite nerve-wracking, but somehow it all came together in the end.

Within the illustration:

The flowers appear on the earth, and the song of the turtledove is heard in our land.

For see, the winter is past, the rains are over and gone.

Arise, my beloved, and come!

Song of Songs 2:10-12

DEBORAH ESTHER POMPANO 2005

My daughter Rebecca modeled for this woodburning, twirling a lovely silk-screen scarf made by my daughter Rachel. I wanted to create a sense of flowing movement and gracefulness in her hair and in all the shapes to express the joy of spring and new beginnings.

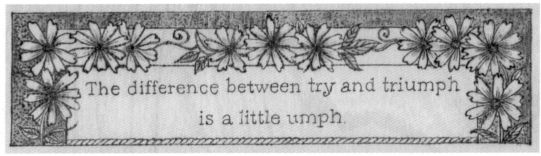

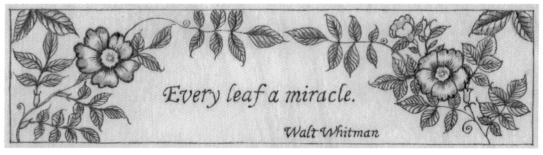

Choose a saying you find inspirational or poignant and create a simple motif to accent it.

INDEX

ACQUISITION EDITOR: Peg Couch

COPY EDITORS: Paul Hambke and Heather Stauffer

COVER AND LAYOUT DESIGNER: Lindsay Hess

COVER AND GALLERY PHOTOGRAPHER: Scott Kriner

DEVELOPMENTAL EDITOR: Michael Degan

EDITOR: Kerri Landis

INDEXER: Jay Kreider

PROOFREADER: Lynda Jo Runkle

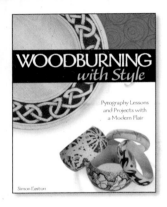

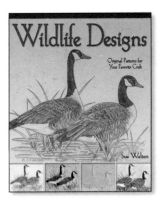
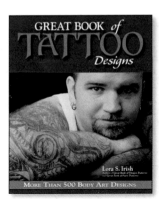